AMYNTAS

ECCO Travels

Smara: The Forbidden City by Michel Vieuchange

Italian Hours by Henry James

Amyntas by André Gide

Pictures from Italy by Charles Dickens

Forthcoming:

The Journey's Echo by Freya Stark

Augustus Hare in Italy

ANDRÉ GIDE

AMYNTAS

Mopsus

Wayside Pages

Biskra to Touggourt

Travel Foregone

TRANSLATED FROM THE
FRENCH BY RICHARD HOWARD
WITH AN AFTERWORD

THE ECCO PRESS
NEW YORK

First published, in French, in 1906
Copyright © 1926 by Éditions Gallimard

Translation copyright © 1988 by Richard Howard
All rights reserved
First published in 1988 by The Ecco Press
26 West 17th Street, New York, N.Y. 10011

Published simultaneously in Canada by
Penguin Books Canada Ltd., Ontario

Printed in the United States of America
Designed by Beth Tondreau Design

LIBRARY OF CONGRESS CATALOGING-IN-PUBLICATION DATA
Gide, André, 1869–1951.
[Amyntas. English]
Amyntas/André Gide: translated from the French
by Richard Howard with an afterword.
p.   cm. — (Ecco travelers)
ISBN 0-88001-165-3(cloth)
ISBN 0-88001-166-1(paper)
1. Gide, André, 1869–1951—Journeys—Africa, North.
2. Authors, French—20th century—Journeys—Africa, North.
3. Algeria—Description and travel.
4. Tunisia—Description and travel.
I. Title.   II. Series.
PQ2613.I2Z46313 1988
848'.91203—dc19
[B]   87-29618
CIP

TO MADELEINE GIDE

CONTENTS

M O P S U S

APRIL 1899

Incipe, Mopse, prior . . .
—Virgil

I

El Kantara

. . . The crag which since morning lengthened beside us opens at last. Here is the portal; we enter.

It is evening; we had been walking in shadow; now the waning day's profusion reappears: lovely, coveted land! what rapture and what repose will your distances bestow, beneath the warm golden light?

We stop; we wait; we look.

A different world appears; alien, motionless, taciturn, bleached. Exultant? no, nor grim: at peace.

We approach; as though into tepid, murky water, beneath the palms, timidly, step by step, we advance . . . Flute notes; a white gesticulation; a sibilant rivulet, and a child's laughter at the water's edge—then nothing; no misgivings, no thoughts. Not even repose: here nothing ever stirs. It is still. —What have I wanted till this day? What had I feared?

I I

Evening comes; the herds return; what we took for peace was merely apathy, torpor; for a moment the astonished oasis shudders, struggles to come alive—an infinitely gentle breath touches the palms; blue smoke rises from each clay dwelling and dissolves the village which, once the herds are in, settles down to sleep, sinks into a night still as death.

I I I

Uninterrupted, life persists: the old man dies without a sound, and the child grows imperceptibly. The village stays the same: no one here wants more—no effort; no novelty.

Within these narrow lanes, no luxury compels such poverty to know itself. Everything abides in its frugal felicity, O simple labor in the fields, age of gold! Then on the doorstep, after dark, to beguile with songs and tales the evening's emptiness . . .

I V

Here, between the stolid pillars of the hall, women are dancing, heavy and tall, not so much lovely as alien, and adorned to excess. They move slowly. The pleasure they sell is a solemn one, secret and powerful as death. Near the café, on a courtyard filled with moonlight or with shadows, each has her door ajar. Their beds are low—you lie down on them as in a grave. Pensive Arabs watch the dancers braid their steps to a music continuous as the sound of running water. A man serves coffee in a tiny cup—so tiny you might think you were drinking oblivion.

V

Of all the Arab cafés, I have chosen the darkest, the one most out of the way. What draws me here? Nothing; the shadows, a graceful body weaving round the room, a song— and not to be seen from outside: the solace of secrecy.

I make no noise coming in; I sit down at once, and in order to attract no attention, I pretend to read; I shall see . . .

But there is nothing. One old Arab asleep in a corner; another singing to himself; under the bench, a dog gnawing on a bone; and the owner's child, near the fire, stirs the ashes to waken an ember and warm my brackish coffee. Time passing here is innocent of hours, yet so perfect is our inoccupation that boredom becomes impossible.

V I

What have I sought till this day? Why did I strive? Now, oh now I know, outside of time, the garden where time comes to rest. A tranquil country, sealed away . . . Arcady! I have found the place of peace.

Here the heedless gesture gleans each moment unpursued; tirelessly the moment recapitulates itself; hour repeats hour, day mirrors day.

Lowing of herds in the evening; three notes drift from the flutes beneath the palms; endless complaint of the wood doves. O nature, purposeless and forbearing, unchanged—thus you smiled at the gentlest of poets; thus you will smile at my devout gaze . . .

This evening I have watched the plants slake their thirst as the channeled water spread, refreshing the gardens. Barefoot in the ditch, a black child was guiding the carefully controlled rivulets: as he opened or closed the tiny sluices set in the clay, each released a puddle at the base of the tree trunk it was assigned to.

I have seen that water rising in the crackled ditches, heavy with earth, tepid, and yellowed by a sunbeam. Then at last the water overflowed, gushing out on all sides, flooding a whole barley field . . .

Claudite jam rivos, pueri; sat prata biberunt.

V I I

The fiery sun has almost dried up the stream. But here, under a vault the foliage makes for it, the wadi flows, deepening its course; farther on, it reappears in sunshine, lethargic on the sandy bank.

. . . Ah, to drench my hands in that clear water! to drink it, and to dip my bare feet into it—to plunge my whole body into it . . . What bliss! Here in the shade, this stream is cool as evening itself. A shifting sunbeam pierces the trellis of leaves and like an arrow thrusts down to the very bottom of the giggling stream, where it caresses a pale patch of sand . . . To swim here!

I want to stretch out naked on the bank; the sand is warm, soft, light. And the sun sears me, stabs me . . . I explode, I dissolve, I evaporate into blue air. Delicious cautery—may so much light absorbed give new fuel to my fever, enrich my fervor, inflame my embrace!

V I I I

Unbuckling our sandals that were filling with sand, we managed with great effort to climb the dune we had reached at last, the one which blocked the horizon.

A shifting dune: we knew, to reach it, what harsh countryside, what dry gullies, what flowerless briars . . . Driven

*toward us by the wind, the sand was blinding; when we had
to clamber up the dune, it gave way under our steps; our feet
sank in, as if we had remained motionless, or as if the whole
dune were receding. And though it was not high, it took us
a long time to reach the top.*

*From the other side of the dune, the countryside was even
vaster, though not quite the same. Exhausted, we sat down in
a fold of shade, a little out of the wind. At the very top of the
dune, that wind which lifted and dropped the sand kept
altering the crest line.*

*Around us, above us, on top of each thing, delicate as a
silence, we heard the whisper of sand falling. Soon it had
covered us . . . We went back.*

I X

*The road, in shadow and patches of sun, snakes between the
walled gardens.*

*Praise to the clay walls, overwhelmed by the profusion of
the groves—low walls, unheeded by the branch of apricots
which thrusts out, far out, overhanging my path. Earthen
walls! above you sway the leaning palms, shading my path.
From grove to grove above my path, ignoring these crumbling
walls! wood doves flutter back and forth. Through a breach,
a vine shoot creeps, straightens, and climbs the palm trunk;*

*coils round it, embraces it, grips, reaches an apricot tree,
clings there, sways, falls back, divides, and spreads its broad
leaves. How long is it till that scorching season, when a
slender child shinnies up the tree and hands down, to slake
my thirst, a heavy cluster he has torn free?*

*. . . Clay walls, never wearisome, yet will you not yield at
last? I skirt your shade. A rivulet hugs the wall. The wall fills
the path with shade. In the grove I hear the sound of laughter,
words . . . O lovely grove! And suddenly the water vanishes:
piercing the wall, it ventures into the garden; in its course a
sunbeam finds it—the grove is filled with light.*

*Earthen walls! detested walls! my endless desire besieges
you; a day will come when I shall enter too!*

X

*Recessed in the earthen wall, a low wooden door is hidden.
We shall come to this little door, to which a child holds the
key; we shall lower our heads, make ourselves small to enter
in . . . Ah! we shall say—ah! this is a peaceful place. We had
not known such peace could be found, and a place of such
calm on earth . . . Bring us flutes and milk—we shall lie down
here on straw mats; some palm wine and dates—we shall stay
here till evening. A light breeze makes its way through the
palms; the shade wavers; the sun laughs; beneath the huge*

apricot trees the yellowish water in the ditches turns blue; the fig trees creep along the ground, but what delights us most is the grace of the oleanders.

No moving: let time close over us like water, like a pool into which we have thrown a pebble; the commotion we made upon entering fades away like ripples on the pool: over this world, let the even surface of time close once again.

X I

We had got up very early this morning, so that before the heat began we might cover great distances. O how far the oasis stretches—interminably! How far must we walk between the garden walls? I know that near the edge of the oasis, all these walls come to an end, and the path hesitates between the separate trunks of the palms. Gradually they disperse, as if they were lingering, or discouraged. More forlornly, their skimpier fronds sway overhead . . . A few more. Between them, the countryside opens out. The oasis is over. Nothing more separates our eye from the empty horizon.

Stop here! The great desert unfurls: stop here. Look, over that motionless auburn sea, motionless oases float like islands.

Behind us, the patch of scorching crag that blocks the north winds; sometimes a cloud passes, a white tuft; hesitates, frays out until it is absorbed by the blue air. Farther on, above the warm wall behind us, the mountain, over which the wind streams. *And ahead of us, nothing—the desert's variegated void.*

X I I

Mopsus to Menalcus

If Damon weeps for Daphnis still, if Gallus mourns for Lycoris even now—let them come here; I shall guide their footsteps to oblivion. Here there is nothing to feed their grief; a great calm upon their thoughts. Here life is more voluptuous and more futile, and death itself less difficult.

WAYSIDE PAGES

MARCH–APRIL
1896

Three years ago last autumn, our arrival in Tunis was a wonderful thing. Though already spoiled by the great boulevards which had been cut through it, the city was still classically lovely, harmoniously uniform, and its white-washed houses seemed to glow tenderly in the evening air, like alabaster lamps.

Once you left the French harbor, there was not a single tree to be seen; you had to seek shade in the souks, those great marketplaces, vaulted or roofed with planks and canvas; into them filtered no more than a reflected light, creating a special atmosphere; these souks seemed subterranean, a second city within the city—and nearly as huge as a third of Tunis. From the high terrace where Paul Laurens would go to paint, you saw, looking down to the sea, only a stairway of white terraces intersected by ditchlike courtyards where the women's labor was hung. Evenings, all that white was mauve, and the sky the color of tea roses; mornings, the white turned pink against a faintly violet sky. But after the winter rains, these walls sprout; green moss covers them, and the edge of the terraces resembles the rim of a flower basket.

I missed the white, serious, classical Tunis of that autumn, which reminded me, evenings, as I wandered through its grid of streets, of the Helen of the second part of Faust, or of Psyche, "the agate lamp within thy hand," wandering down a lane of sepulchers. Trees are being planted in the broad streets and on the squares. Tunis will be more attractive because of them, but nothing could disfigure the city more. Two years ago, the Rue Marr and the Place des Moutons were still impossible to identify— where had you been transported?—and the remotest Orient, the most secret Africa, offered no more intoxicating flavor of foreignness. Here was a different form of life, one conducted entirely out of doors, very rich, ancient, classical, fixed: no compromise as yet between the Eastern civilizations and ours, which seems especially ugly when it tries to restore. Tin sheets or leaves of zinc are gradually replacing the reed wattles which roof the souks, and street lamps patchily distribute light on walls where lately the nights' unbroken glow was spread—on that vast Place des Moutons, without sidewalks, silent, wonderful, where only two years ago, in the warmth of the moonlight, Arabs came to sleep beside their herds of camels.

Sidewalks have been laid in the souks; in one of the finest colonnades, the pedestals of the little pillars support-ing the vault have been covered up—twisted pillars, green and red, with massive, carved capitals. The vault is white-washed, but scantily lit. Even on the most brilliant days, these souks are always half dark.

The entrance to the souks is a wonderful place; I am not referring to the mosque portico, but to that other entrance, narrow and recessed, sheltered by a jujube tree which bends down and offers a shadowy prelude to the dim alley-way, swerving sharply and immediately lost to view. But the jujube tree, covered with leaves in autumn, still has none this spring. It is the saddle-makers' souk which be-gins here; the lane turns, then continues interminably.

In the perfume souk, Sadouk-Anoun is always seated cross-legged in his stall, no more than a niche, its floor on trestles, cluttered with bottles and flasks; but the perfumes he sells today are artificial ones. I gave Paul Valéry, when I returned to Paris, the last two authentic flasks, which I saw Sadouk-Anoun himself siphon full of apple essence and precious ambergris, drop by drop. He no longer so carefully seals them, half full of a more ordinary stock, with beeswax and white thread, and no longer charges me so much for them. Three years ago, his meticulosity de-lighted us; it seemed to give things a higher value. With each sachet he added, the scent became more exquisite. Finally we made him stop—our purse was no longer sufficient.

And in vain I have searched for that dim café patronized exclusively by tall black men from the Sudan. Some were missing one toe—a sign of servitude. Most of them were wearing, stuck beneath their turban, a tiny tuft of white flowers, fragrant jasmine; this bouquet falls against the cheek like a romantic lock of hair and gives their face an expression of voluptuous languor. They so prize the scent of these flowers that sometimes, not satisfied to inhale the odor, they thrust the crumpled petals far into their nostrils. —In this café, one of them was singing, another telling stories; and doves were fluttering back and forth, landing on their shoulders.

Tunis, March 7

Little children watch this show and laugh, repeating among themselves the obscene gestures of Karaghioz. A difficult gymnastic for the European mind: to train itself to find such things natural . . . An audience of children— nothing but children here, most of them extremely young—what do they make of it?

The French never come here; they don't know where to go, cannot find such places; these are tiny, unrewarding-looking stalls; you make your way in through a low door. The French usually patronize the showy establishment next door, which makes a lot of noise and attracts only tourists; the Arabs know whom to trust, and that there is not much to a dancing cardboard horse, or a wood-and-canvas camel which also dances—very entertainingly, it is true, but in a fairground fashion. And close by, there is a traditional Karaghioz stall, classic, simple—it could hardly be simpler, an admirable stage convention, where Karaghioz hides in the center of the stage, between two gendarmes looking for him, simply because he ducks his head and can no longer see *them;* and the children accept this, understand, laugh . . .

Karaghioz. —A narrow room, a market stall by day, which is taken down in the evening; a tiny stage, a curtain of translucent canvas is set up at the back for the shadow puppets. Perpendicular to the stage, two benches along the walls. These are the best seats. The middle of the room fills with very young children who sit on the ground, poking one another. Huge amounts of dried, salted melon seeds are devoured, a delicacy so alluring that each evening my pocket is emptied, which I have filled each morning for two sous. It must be admitted that I give the children some.

What is fun here are those niches up in the wall, each holding a sort of very uncomfortable little divan—kingfisher's nests to which you have to shinny up and from which you do not climb down—you tumble down; these are rented only for the whole evening, to young aficionados. Here I returned many evenings—it was nearly always the same audience, in the same seats, listening to the same plays, and laughing at the same places—like myself.

Karaghioz. —Another stall; Sudanese here. Where the Sudanese are, Arabs are reluctant to go. So here you see only black faces. But this evening I also find my friend R. once again.

The play hasn't begun. (The intermissions are always much longer than the play; this one lasts no more than fifteen minutes). A black man rattles castanets, another thumps an oblong drum, and the third—a huge fellow— flaps and dandles in front of R.; sitting almost at our feet, he sings, improvising a monotonous chant in which he observes, so far as I can make out, that he is very poor, that R. is very rich, and that black men always need money. And since he seems rather fierce, and the Arabs claim that you cannot trust either a camel, a black man, or the desert for long, we lose no time in becoming very charitable.

Karaghioz. —Another stall. Here, the play is merely an excuse for encounters. Always the same habitués, evening after evening, under the owner's benevolent gaze. A strangely lovely child plays the bagpipes: people gather around him; the others are his suitors. Another plays that strange jug-shaped drum made of donkey skin. The bagpiper makes the café's fortune, seeming to smile at all and to favor none. Some recite verses to him—sing them, actually; he answers, approaches, but I suspect it all comes down to a few very public flatteries; this stall is not a brothel, but a kind of *cour d'amour*. Sometimes one of them gets up and dances, sometimes two; the dancing then becomes a rather risqué sort of pantomime.

The play, here as elsewhere, is almost always obscene. I'd like to know the history of Karaghioz—he must be very old; I am told he came from Constantinople and that everywhere else except in Constantinople and in Tunis the police have forbidden his performances; he is to be seen only during Ramadan, when there is fasting for forty days from sunrise to sunset; a complete fast—neither food, nor drink, nor tobacco, nor perfumes, nor women. All the senses, chastised by day, take their revenge after dark, and one seeks whatever diversion one can find. Of course there are also very religious Arabs, who spend their Ramadan nights, after a very frugal meal, in meditation and prayer; just as there are others who continue to seek entertainment even by day; but this is common only in big cities which the roumis have depraved; in general Arabs, almost all of them, are scrupulously observant.

This last evening I wanted to see once more, before leaving, everything richest and strangest that Tunis had shown me. I recall being haunted for a long time by a marching-band of soldiers returning to their barracks—very loud, precise, and victorious—while here and there, on the harbor and along the French boulevards, Bengal lights changed the branches of the peppertrees into an uncertain pink filigree.

Only a few Arabs turned to glance at this little procession; the high-pitched music of their cafés persisted.

Many of them recall, I suppose, the first day that triumphant music entered their conquered city. I wondered if their thoughts did not still harbor, for the French, a good measure of hatred.

I sought my pleasure the length of the Rue Marr; but I kept regretting the Halfaouïne. One Moorish cafe was quite large, quite fine, but I was only half-tolerated there. The French never come. The animation of the Halfaouïne attracts them; the other neighborhoods remain silent. An old black man began dancing, quite grotesquely, to the sounds of the bagpipe, to the rhythm of the drum.

Along the dim boulevards, I returned to the Halfaouïne. Not a big crowd; nothing special. Toward the evening's end, I ran into R. once again, in the same Karaghioz stall I had taken him to the first day. He too realizes the advantage of returning regularly to the same places in order to recognize not many faces, but to know them and not just to see them pass by. The Arabs grow used to you, you seem less foreign to them, and their routine, disturbed at first, resumes.

El Kantara

We reached here at the end of a splendid day. Athman had arrived this morning, had napped a little during the afternoon, but was at the station waiting for us the last hour. How long that hour seemed to him! "And yet," he told me, "I was thinking: only an hour; before, it was a whole year . . ."

Three burnooses; a gandoura of white silk lined with blue and piped with flesh pink; a jacket of pastel-blue canvas; the huge turban of brown rope squeezing the fine white stuff which drops below, brushes the cheek, and floats under the chin. This headgear transforms him; last year, at sixteen, he wore only the simple child's chechia; at seventeen he insists on the men's complicated turban. Athman has spent all he has on his outfit; he has dressed up for our reunion. Without his greeting, I should hardly have known him.

The evening fell slowly; we had crossed the gorge, and the fabulous Orient calmly showed itself in all its irenic gilding. We went down under the palm trees, leaving Athman to wait on the road for the carriage which was to meet us. I recognized every sound—of the running water, of the birds. Everything was just as before, at peace; our arrival had changed nothing.

In the carriage, we skirted the oasis—a good long ride. On our way back, the sun was setting and we got out at the doorway of a Moorish café, once the hour of Ramadan had passed. In the courtyard, quite close to us, some rutting camels were fighting, their keeper screaming at them. The flock of goats was returning for the night.

From each of the gray earth houses rose a thin column of smoke which soon enveloped and blurred the whole oasis in a blue vapor. The sky, in the west, was a very pure blue, so transparent that it still seemed filled with light. The silence became wonderful; you could not imagine any song here. I felt I loved this place more than any other, perhaps . . .

Biskra

Yesterday, we were in the gardens: we followed the lanes which at first led us to N'Msid, then to Bab el Derb. We reached the old fort, and returned by way of Sidi Barkat. The excursion was a long one, and Madeleine was tired by it. —Athman was with us, and R.; Larbi followed. We stopped in the café on the edge of N'Msid that overlooks the wadi bed, Laliah, the Aurès mountains.

I am not so taken with this landscape as, on the other side, the blank expanse of the desert. Larbi was playing dominoes with us, cheating and charming. I was waiting for Jammes with a delicious impatience. The earth here speaks a different tongue, but one I understand by now.

My room, last year, was on the ground floor of the hotel; my open window, elbow high, was all that separated me from outdoors; one could easily slip over the sill. Sadek, Athman's older brother, and a few others from old Biskra, during Ramadan, used to visit my room before returning to their village. I had dates, cookies, things to drink, sweets. Night had fallen. Sadek would play the flute, and we managed to stay silent for a long time.

At night, I closed only the shutters: all the sounds from outdoors came into the room. Each morning they wakened me before dawn, and I would go to the edge of the desert to watch the sunrise. At that moment Lassif's flock passed, comprising the poor folk's goats, for since these villagers had no garden they entrusted their animals to him every morning; Lassif took them out to the desert to graze. From door to door, before dawn, he made his way, knocking at each; the door would open and release a few goats which followed him. By the time he left the village, he had more than sixty.

He went a long way with them, toward the hot spring, where chokeweed and the euphorbia grow. There was one big billy goat he rode sometimes, when the way was tiring, or else to divert himself, for he did not know how to play the flute. One morning when he had left without passing my window, I set out for the desert to join him.

I love the desert more than anything else. The first year,

I was a little afraid of it because of the wind, because of the sand; then, not having any goal, I didn't know how to stop, and I quickly exhausted myself. I came to prefer the shady paths under the palms, the groves of Ouardi, the villages. But last year I began taking immense walks, with no other purpose than to lose sight of the oasis. I would walk—I walked until I felt myself immensely alone in that vast expanse. Then I began to look. The sands had velvety touches of shadow under each hillock; there were wonderful rustlings in every breath of wind; because of the great silence, the least sound could be heard. Sometimes an eagle soared over the great dunes. This monotonous expanse seemed to me, day by day, of a more plausible diversity.

I knew the nomad shepherds; I would go out to meet them, would talk to them; some could play the flute deliciously. Occasionally I would sit with them a long time, doing nothing at all; I would always bring a book, but almost never opened it. I often came back only at evening. But Athman, to whom I described these excursions, told me that they were unwise, and that prowling Arabs haunt the outskirts of the oasis and plunder helpless foreigners; it would have been their profession to attack me. From that day, he insisted on accompanying me; but since he didn't enjoy walking, my excursions grew shorter and shorter, then ceased altogether.

. . .

Athman reads like Bouvard and writes like Pécuchet. He is learning with all his might, and copies anything he can get his hands on. He prefers Hérold's *Joie de Maguelonne* to my *Tentative amoureuse,* which he finds poorly written. "You use the word 'grass' too often," he tells me.

I give him the *Thousand and One Nights.* One night, he takes the book to Bordj Boulakras, where he sleeps, to read it with his friend Bachaga. The next day he doesn't appear until ten, still numb with sleep; he and his friend had been reading the story of Aladdin until two in the morning, he explains; and adds: "Oh yes, we spent a good *nocturnal night.*" Nocturnal, to him, means waking.

At the edge of the oasis, as we pass the deserted ruins of the old fort on this moonlit night, white-clad Arabs are lying on the ground, talking in low voices, and one is murmuring into a flute. "They are going to spend a nocturnal night," Athman tells me, "telling each other stories." In summer, you would not dare lie down on the ground—scorpions and horned adders, hidden during the day in the sand, come out and hunt after dark. After a while we leave the carriage; there are no more palms here; the night seems to extend the desert to the edge of its blue brilliance. Even Jammes has nothing to say. And all at once Athman, overcome by a lyrical impulse, sheds his burnoose, wriggles out of his gandoura, and turns cartwheels in the moonlight.

. . .

Athman has found some "Lives of Notable Men"—and now, apropos of the camels, he quotes Buffon or Cuvier, and no longer mentions friendship without citing Henri IV and Sully, or courage without Bayard, and the Great Bear without Galileo.

He writes to Degas, sending him a palm-stem cane; he says, "I'm glad that you don't like Jews, that you read *La Libre Parole,* and that you agree with me that Poussin is a great French painter."

Jammes delights in making him read out loud these verses he has improvised while we wait for the carriage which will take us to Droh:

To my friend Athman

My dear friend Athman
the trees that bear almonds
fig trees and currant bushes
are good for sitting under
when you are very tired

You rest there without moving
and keep your eyes closed.
It is good to be lazy.
In the groves, you hear
the clear water singing
like an Arab woman.

It is good to do nothing
and keep your eyes closed
as if you were asleep.
So good here, Athman,
in this great indolence
that you think you are dead.

Ever since Jammes has come, Athman spends night and day making verses. Sometimes he comes up with real finds:

Under the palms, there are no concerts . . .

or again:

. . . One who knows
love has drunk a bitter drink
and time is out of mind.

But I am afraid they occur, for the most part, by accident. Besides, he is only seventeen.

He still is assiduously reading the *Thousand and One Nights,* knows the story of Aladdin by heart, and now signs his letters:

ATHMAN
OR THE MAGIC LAMP

Jammes gives me his cane. It is made of ironwood and comes from the "Islands." It delights the children here because the handle is a greyhound's head; it is polished like jade, and yet so crude that it seems to be whittled. I've never seen anything so odd. Down the shaft, there are verses in capital letters, including these:

> A squirrel had a
> rose in its teeth, a donkey
> called him crazy.

And these, which he used to put at the top of all his letters:

> A bee sleeps
> in the thickets of my heart.

Touggourt, April 7

Today they are decorating an Arab well-digger.

Before the drilling companies came, and the artesian crews, the Arabs had well-diggers. Sometimes they have to find springs seventy or eighty meters below the surface. Men actually climb down into the holes; they have been trained since boyhood for this arduous profession, but many of them die in its performance. They must penetrate three layers of earth and two of water—the first stagnant, the second merely seeping—to reach that last gushing layer. The water wells up then, sometimes admirably clear and abundant, but almost always full of sodium nitrate and magnesium. The effort of these well-diggers, working under the water layer, is inconceivable; here was one of the bravest and strongest, I was told. He has bored through the water layer, making a passage which the water cannot penetrate and in which he can work, digging deeper, and this twice over, through two liquid layers, to establish a conduit for the fresh water which must, without being contaminated, gush up through the stagnant water.

The same day, in one of these four-sided holes formed of palm trunks, we saw a man go down, hanging from a rope—sixty meters deep—to repair a leak.

So, they have decorated the Arab well-digger; that evening, he went mad.

The layer of stagnant water, in Touggourt, is just below the surface. These are no longer the fine freshwater springs of Chetma or the trickling canals of Biskra, these are stagnant, stinking ditches filled with nasty weeds; however, a river crosses the oasis as well, cunningly divided to irrigate the groves. Out there, among the weeds, creep the water snakes.

The oasis is ringed by the sands; yesterday, a dreadful storm raised them; the horizon seemed to fall back upon

us like a blanket being folded up; we could see nothing—
we could scarcely breathe.

Not far from the town is a wretched cemetery which the
sand is slowly invading; you can still make out a few
graves. In the desert the notion of death pursues you, yet
wonderfully enough, it is not melancholy here. In Biskra,
behind the old fort, in the very center of the oasis, the rains
have gullied the old cemetery, and since the dead are
buried directly in the earth, the scattered bones there are
as abundant, in places, as pebbles.

The sandstorm lasted till evening; at sunset, we went up
the minaret: the palms were leaden and the town panting
under an ashen sky.

A huge wind came out of the east like a breath of divine
malediction heralded by the prophets. And in this desolation, we saw a caravan *vanishing.*

The Ouleds here dance better than at Biskra, and they
are more beautiful; in fact it is only here that I have seen
them dance well. We returned, insatiable, to that solemn,
lingering dance, all arms and wrists, very proper—dazed,
almost stunned by that stubborn, swift, evasive, intoxicating music which induces ecstasy and never falls silent when
you leave it—and which still haunts me certain evenings,
like the desert itself.

I would have liked to spend the night in the place where
those caravans were encamped. Brush fires were set;

around them, Arabs were talking in low voices; others were singing; they sang all night.

Athman tells me the story of Uriah's wife. According to the Arab tradition, it was while hunting a golden dove from hall to hall of his palace, that David, whom he calls Daoud, finally reached that high terrace from which Bathsheba could be seen.

Athman's version: ". . . the Jew tells him that Moses was right and that God would take to Himself first the Jews, then the Arabs, and perhaps even the Christians. The Christian tells him that Christ was right and that God would take the Christians to Himself, but the Arabs too, and even the Jews. The Arab tells him that Mohammed was right and that God would take the Arabs into His paradise, but that He would close the gates to Jews and Christians who had not converted. And when he had heard all three, he lost no time in becoming a Moslem."

The Christians have the privileges of seniority; Arabs believe, or so they tell me, that a Christian, if he utters before dying the Credo of Islam: "God is God, Mohammed is His prophet," will enter Paradise *before* an Arab.

"The roumis," they also say, "are superior to us in many things; but they are still afraid of death."

Touggourt, April 9

Arabs encamped on the square, fires lit; smoke almost invisible in the evening air. We were on the roof of the mosque when the muezzin climbed up to call the faithful to evening prayer.

The sun was setting as though forever on the interminable, exhausted plain. The sand, pale for hours, had turned darker than the sky.

We had suffered all day from the sun, and the cool of the evening was delectable to us. Children were playing in the square, and dogs were barking on the terraces of the houses. Above us the muezzin's voice filled the little cupola which surmounts the minaret; extended on a single note, it produced a droning echo; then suddenly it stopped, leaving a void in the air.

Because of the extraordinary drought, all the cattle died this year, and meat has become so rare that people are reduced to eating camel.

On the way out of town, you see, under a little roof of dried palm fronds, one of these huge half-dismembered creatures, the violet flesh covered by flies as soon as you stop driving them off. The flies in this country are as numerous as the seed of Abraham. They lay their eggs on the abandoned carcasses—of sheep, horses, or camels—that are left to rot in the sun; the larvae feed here freely and then, transformed, come to the towns in swarms, in hordes. You swallow them, you breathe them, you are tickled, tormented, blinded by them; the walls hum with them, the butcher stalls and the grocer's shops sputter. In Touggourt, each merchant, waving a tiny palm broom, tries to send them to his neighbor. In Kairouan, there are so many that it is best to leave them be. The vendors do not wave them off except when a customer asks to see the merchandise. Our carriage, arriving, was shrouded in a cloud of them. At the hotel, the plates and glasses were protected by metal lids which were raised only when you were actually going to eat or drink.

M' Reyer, April 11

Amazing salt lakes, the chotts rimmed with mirages; from the top of a sandy hill, after the vast extent of desert, you think: "That must be the sea!" A vast blue sea with skiffs and islands, a sea you hope is a deep one, and your soul is refreshed by it! You approach, you touch the brim, and suddenly the blue vanishes—it was no more than the sky's reflection on a salt surface fiery to touch, painful to look at, and yielding underfoot, the thin, fragile crust of a sea of moving mud in which whole caravans are engulfed.

At an officer's mess, the major beside me tells me about the South. For a long time he lived at Ouargla; he actually came from El-Goléah, and remembered the soldiers' trek through the desert. Often, in these shifting, scorching, shimmering sands, a special kind of dizziness overcame the men, so that they kept feeling the ground soften underfoot, even when they had come to a halt. Sometimes then, in the midst of the painful sands, they came upon a narrow seam of calcareous rock, something agglomerated, hard, and just broad enough for each soldier in turn to rest both feet on it and momentarily recover his balance by means of that slight resistance.

To punish a soldier, he was made to "follow": to walk behind the ranks is murderous; those in front cannot bother about the laggards; sometimes they string out that way . . . staggering, falling, swallowed up by the desert. The last ones run in the smothering dust which the ranks have raised, on that soft sand all the softer for having been trampled by all the rest. If a man loses his footing, he's done for; he watches the others disappearing, and rests; the birds flying behind the line of march stop, wait—then approach.

In this sand, the gypsum crystals, debris of *fer-de-lances*, often shine like mica. On the Droh road, we found stones which, broken open, look transparent inside, as though they were empty.

On the El Oued road, we gathered some of those strange

mineral flowers called "Souf roses," which are nothing but a little conglutinated gray sand.

Biskra

The sounds of the Negro drum attract us. Negro music! how often I heard it during the past year! How often I got up to follow it! No tones, just rhythm; no melodic instrument, nothing but percussion—long drums, tom-toms and castanets . . .

"Florentes ferulas et grandia lilia quassens," castanets which produce, in their hands, the noise of a clattering shower. With three musicians, they perform rhythmic wonders; strangely syncopated rhythms which madden you and provoke all kinds of bodily reflexes. These are musicians who play in funeral ceremonies, which are also joyous and deeply religious; I have seen them, in the cemeteries, sustain the mourners' intoxication; in a Kairouan mosque, exasperate the mystic madness of the Aïssaouas; in the little mosque of Sidi-Malek, I have seen them keep time to the dance of the staves and to the sacred dances; and I was always the only Frenchman watching. I don't know where the tourists go; I suspect that the official guides work up a phony Africa for them, in order to divert the importunate from the Arabs, who love secrecy and peace, for I never met any of my coun-

trymen where anything interesting was going on, nor
even, fortunately, in the ancient villages of the oasis,
where I returned each day and ended by no longer trou-
bling anyone. Yet the hotels are filled with travelers; but
they fall into the hands of charlatan guides, and pay a lot
to watch fake ceremonies staged for them.

Nor was there a single Frenchman, last year, at that
extraordinary night festival which I attended almost by
chance, lured by the mere sound of the tom-tom and by the
wailing of the women. The festival was in the Negro village;
a dancing procession of women and musicians was making
its way up the main street, ahead of torchbearers and a
group of children laughing and leading by the horns a huge
black goat, covered with jewels and garlands. He had rings
on his horns, an enormous silver loop in his nostrils, and
necklaces around his neck; he was wrapped in a rag of
crimson silk. In the crowd that followed, I recognized tall
Ashour; he explained that this goat would be slaughtered
during the night to bring luck to the village; he was
paraded through the streets beforehand so that the wicked
house-spirits, which hover on the doorsteps, would enter
into him and vanish.

Negro music! how many times, far from Africa, I imag-
ined I heard you and suddenly the whole South was re-
created around me; in Rome once, in the Via Gregoriana,
heavy wagons rolling through the city at dawn awakened

me. At the sound of those heavy echoes on the cobble-stones, and still half asleep, I could deceive myself a moment—then regret my error at length.

We heard it this morning, that Negro music, but not for any ordinary festivity: they were playing in the inner court-yard of a private house, and men on the doorstep tried to keep us out at first, but several Arabs recognized me and made it possible for us to go in. I was amazed, first of all, by the great number of Jewish women there—very beautiful, almost all of them, and richly dressed. The courtyard was full; there was scarcely any space left in the middle for dancing. The dust and heat were asphyxiating. A great shaft of light fell from the upper bay, where, as from a balcony, clusters of children were leaning down.

The staircase up to the terrace was also filled with people; everyone was watching very closely, and soon we were too. In the center of the courtyard was a huge copper basin filled with water. Three women stood up—three Arab women; they stripped off their upper garments for the dance, loosened their hair in front of the basin, then, leaning over, spread their hair on the water. The music, already very loud, swelled louder still; letting their sopping hair drip down their bodies, the women began to dance; this was a fierce, frenzied dance, and unless you had seen it, you could have no idea what it was like. An old black woman presided, leaping around the basin and striking its

rim every once in a while with a stick she held in one hand.
We were told, later, what we were beginning to guess: that
all the women dancing that day (and sometimes there were
so many that two days were needed) were possessed—both
Jews and Arabs.

Each in her turn paid to be allowed to dance. That old
black woman with the stick was a famous witch, who knew
the exorcisms; stirring up the water in the basin, she urged
each demon to dive in, thereby releasing the victim.

All this was explained to us by the lovely Jewess Goumarr'ha, who spoke somewhat reluctantly, constrained by
a vestige of belief and a certain shame in confessing that
last year she too, suffering horribly from hysteria, had
taken part in the dance, "hoping to find in it a relief from
her sufferings." But afterward, she had grown much worse,
and her husband, learning that she had danced at this
witches' sabbath, had beaten her for three days in order to
cure her.

. . . The dance grew wilder; the haggard, frantic women
seeking release from the flesh, or better still loss of feeling, achieved that crisis where, their bodies escaping all
control of their minds, the exorcism could function. After
the immediate fatigue, sweating, swooning in the self-
annihilation which follows the crisis, they might find
peace.

Now they are kneeling before the basin, their hands

clutching its rim and their bodies flung from right to left, back and forth, like a frenzied pendulum; their hair whips the water, then spatters their shoulders; with each contraction of their loins, they utter a deep cry, like that of woodcutters chopping; then suddenly they collapse backward as if into epileptic fits, foaming at the lips, hands rigid. The evil spirit has left them.

Then the witch stretches out their bodies, dries them, rubs them, spreads their limbs, and as we do for hysterics, grasping them by the wrists and pulling them to a seated posture, presses the lower part of their bellies with her foot or her knee. More than sixty of them, we were told, had been put through this ceremony that day. The first ones were still writhing, while others were already flinging themselves into the dance. One was tiny and hunchbacked, wearing a yellow and green gandoura. She leapt about like the sprite in some tale, her coal-black hair covering her from head to foot.

The Jewesses danced as well. They bounced about chaotically, like delirious dolls; they leapt up only once to fall back at once, distracted. Others showed more resistance, but their madness was contagious—we fled the place, unable to endure it any longer.

Biskra

"Who invented music?" Athman asks. I answer: "Musicians." He is not satisfied; he insists on an answer. I answer solemnly that it was God.

"No," he says at once, "it was the devil." And he explains to me that for Arabs, all musical instruments are instruments of hell, with the exception of the two-stringed viol, whose name I cannot remember, the one with a very long neck and a sound box made of a tortoiseshell. This is played with a little bow, and accompanies the singers in the square, poets, prophets, and storytellers, sometimes so sweetly, Athman says, that a doorway to paradise seems to open.

These singers, these poets intrigue me. What do they sing? And the goatherds, in dialogue with the flute? And Sadek with his gusla? And Athman himself, alone or with Ahmed, each on his horse, in Touggourt? I listen, but I cannot make out a single word. Athman, whom I question, answers: "No, of course not—there are no sentences—it's just poetry!" By insisting, I manage, the last few days, to make him transcribe and translate a few of these songs. These are the ones sung by the singers in the squares, sitting on the ground, or on the doorstep of a café, surrounded by a group of silent, listening Arabs; or the ones they sing to themselves, in the solitude of long journeys. I don't know if they will please those unfamiliar with the country; all I can claim is that I myself find them very beautiful, and believe the oral tradition of this Arabic poetry, ancient and modern, is worthy of a place in the world's folklore. Here are two of these songs; I give them as Athman gave them to me, correcting only the spelling:

I

For two years I stopped making love and said
    I was a holy man.
I made my journey to the North; I found
    in the festival, Baya . . .
She set a comb in her hair and jewels in her ears,
and the dagger, with the mirror . . .
Her hair falls on all sides,
weighted with gold, carefully braided.
No one can buy her
No one but her or me . . .
—The girls have asked for coins
And I, a weak man (I am poor),
Tomorrow I shall sell a few sheep
For the beauties with their fine jewels.

II

Today, as she passed, she turned around,
with a golden belt, the fringes hanging

over her thighs
—what makes me suffer is her white dress—
I shall spend all night running,
and it is I who makes the dogs howl.*

If Ramadan were a man,
I myself would break his knees,
But Ramadan has come from God,
you and I accept its sufferings.

*Love is very difficult with us, Athman says, explaining the poem, because the women are protected by dogs and by the whole family.

BISKRA TO TOUGGOURT

DECEMBER 1900

for Madeleine Gide

I copy out here—for whom else but you?—these faded notes. It was for you that I wrote them in the interminable tedium of the journey, after leaving you in Biskra. That charabanc which every four days covers the postal route between Biskra and Touggourt passes in front of the hotel well before dawn. I can still see our farewells, on the terrace, in the dark . . .

I

Tuesday, 5 o'clock

Still in the oasis. —A gentle glow, so pale that the light already seems shadow and the shadow darkness. A morning moonlight in which the dawn will dissolve.

A roadside cemetery—where Athman's parents are lying, under the glacial calm of these nights. Only the white graves of the marabouts glisten; then, faintly, the other

graves, earth-color, mingle their dust with the night. Palm
trees border the cemetery; at their foot, the water in the
seguias shimmers under the moon as we pass. No song, no
scent, no sound; the somber poetry of this place, of this
hour, consists in just this mortal destitution.

The road passes through the village. Everything is
asleep. In the ash-gray houses, not a single lamp, not a
single fire.

Do you remember that on our last journey, at this hour
and in this place, on the ruined wall of the mosque, a tiny
owl was hooting, undisturbed by our approach but quite
solemnly watching us watching it.

Then the last palm trees thin out; and that dubious
dream of life that was the sleeping oasis abandons us to the
desert, to the night, to death.

Yet far away, infinitely distant, a few fires, three or
four—a nomad camp, where the caravans stop.

Not one cloud in the blue, where the dawn will soon
appear. The East is violet and melancholy, like a bruise on
the night.

We pass a caravan coming toward us. The moon, almost
at the zenith, grants each camel no more than a brief,
discreet shadow. It is cold. Athman, in Arab fashion, pulls
his huge turban into the three hoods of his burnoose,

hunches down, rounds his shoulders, and becomes a gourd, like the Emperor Claudius.

The salt-silvered plain gleams faintly under the moon: magnesia or sodium nitrate, I don't know which; the smooth silver-frosted ground seems a liquid substance. And scattered here and there upon it, a cluster of mastic trees, a tuft of slender reeds.

Not one cloud. And now the dawn: from the night's still-cold azure to the red rim of the sands occurs a prismatic analysis of the daylight, more delicately and more subtly nuanced, but also more precisely detailed, than that of a perfect rainbow; and on the awestruck earth, a resurrection of colors. All with a total absence of art, with a beauty purely and solely natural.

This will last only a moment. Already every subtle nuance is fading; nothing must remain in space but the brutal gold and the blue. But before the sun appears, the sky is once again washed with a strange orange pallor, out of which the sun now appears, flat and red, like a piece of soft iron on the anvil.

7 o'clock

A flight of cranes in the gold sky makes a tremulous oblong cloud. Another, smaller flight follows the first. They approach; we can count them: thirteen. Each of these flights passes on our left. In augural lore, what does this omen mean?

Until Saada, the only living things we encountered were the impassive caravans. Oh yes, two jackals. The first ran away, frightened by our approach. The other remains quite close to us, motionless and "hidden" behind a low bush; only his pointed muzzle sticks out.

Dawn over the sea has never seemed so splendid to me: where the sands are reddening, trembling, the waves, on the other hand, remain frozen. Then the desert extends, stubbornly changeless. Blond, rather pebbly clay where low round reddish bushes appear, which hold the sand and hoist themselves on top of it; on this smooth surface, they look like an outbreak of warts.

From Saada to Chegga, we have encountered nothing.

Chegga, 10:30

Breakfast—on a three-legged table—under the sun already beginning to blaze. Two starved cats quarrel over the remains of cold chicken and sardines. Near us, in front of the wretched hut where three poor Arabs take shelter, a woman wrapped in a saffron rag washes a skinny girl of five, stark naked, standing in a black cauldron. Not one flower, not one blade of grass to mellow the hut a little.

If you do not know this country, first imagine: nothing. To the right, a hut. Close by, a few dismantled carcasses— camels, I suppose. To the left, a string of camels, their drivers watering them at a spring we cannot see. Behind the well from which the spring emerges, nothing; around us, nothing; sun; an avalanche of sun.

We approach the spring. Why bother! The channeled water trickles into an orchard where twenty skinny palms are withering. A bald donkey crops at the base of one of them; it looks as if he is grazing on the sand. The charabanc harnessed, we set out again.

1 o'clock

For over two hours, the same road unwinds in front of us, thickened now by fine sand. The wheels leave a track; the horses strain; we get down. The sun blazes. The overilluminated plain, as far as the eye can see, seems leaden; all colors die. But if you turn around, putting the sun behind you, the tones revive, and the relation of the low dunes to the scanty vegetation embellishing them is enchanting. I do not know what these plants are called. Their tiny, tense leaves are of a silvery, ashen green, exactly like that of the olive tree.

Kef el Dorh'

Suddenly the terrain slopes down to the salt lake, the chott.

There was a time when I dared not admit to myself how little refuge and sustenance art finds on this land. I needed to claim it was lovely in order to admire it so passionately. That was when I was still quite ready to confuse art and nature. Now, what I love in this country is—I can tell—its actual hideousness, its inclemency: what constrains any art *not* to exist . . . or to take refuge elsewhere.

Here the painter's impotence is conclusive and his stubbornness in not acknowledging it is a joke. In the desert, you must learn to be content with the education—I mean with the exaltation—it proposes, then discover how to counterpoise it. This is precisely what a Monet would have acquired here, I imagine: the analysis of his craft, of his eye; the simplest knowledge of each tone in itself, of its relationships and its possible importance; the disappearance of all planes, the vanishing of reflections, the lack of variegation, the nakedness of the milieu. And, returning

home, he would have acquired—from the interactions of the tones among themselves, from the resources of each, from the readiness of surfaces to reflect, from the ambience itself—a comprehension both more knowing and more spontaneous, a kind of revelation.

M'Reyer

. . . where we arrive in darkness. *Bordj;* a huge courtyard, and how describe its gloom? Nothing here—it is effortlessly huge, for here nothing costs less than space.

As soon as you leave the *bordj,* the night seems so vast that the *bordj* seems tiny in it. Never had I seen so many stars. Wherever you look in the sky, they appear. The dogs howl . . . an indefinable anguish seizes you; —you are poorly protected against the void; everywhere you feel the desert yielding.

Wandering in the dark, we try to reach the village which the carriage, before stopping at the *bordj,* had skirted. It is far away. We hear a barracks tune being sung, then we see four soldiers approaching, offering to guide us. We leave them as soon as we enter the village. It is very cold. In the middle of the street—if that is what this canal between the houses can be called—half-naked children are tending palm fires where old men warm themselves. The flame bursts out a second, sputtering, then falls back, and there is nothing more than the muffled radiance of the embers. No music, no games; a few virtually extinguished Moorish cafés; a few smokers on their doorsteps, half reclining on matting or just on the ground.

And now that we have twice followed the whole length of the only two streets of the village, now that the fires are out, now that we have driven off, like flocks of wild birds, everything young and charming that was warming itself here, now that the peace of this all-too-alien place is ruined—what is there to do but return to the *bordj* through the oppressive solitude of the night?

I I

Wednesday, noon

Gray stripes have appeared in the South; for two hours, the sky has been entirely covered with clouds; then, toward the South again, the blue has reappeared. Now, once more, not a cloud from one edge of the sky to the other.

5 o'clock

We are in sight of Touggourt. The sinking sun reddens. The sky is entirely blue, a blue which turns golden round the edges. The approach to Touggourt exceeds all my recollections. On the horizon to the left, the fine line of the oasis extending from M'garine looks like a gulf coast, and the sandy sea on which we are drifting rises to meet it. To the right, nothing; the gold sand joins the vibrant gold of the sky. Ahead of us, the considerable town of Touggourt.

Belated haven! Still far off, all we see of it, straight ahead, almost outside the oasis, are two strange minarets, silhouetted like lighthouses, black against the sky.

Meanwhile the sun is vanishing. In the East, the sand, pink and green for a second, all at once takes on a delicate pallor, a very fine lividity, exquisite under the pink and lilac sky . . .

TRAVEL
FOREGONE

1903–1904

I was of an age when life begins
to have a suspect taste on the
lips; when you feel each moment
falling from a little lower
place in the past.

Obsessed by a craving for that country, by a desire which, each year, seethed in me as autumn approached, and casting about for some cure—pro remedio animae meae, *I decided to write a book about North Africa.*

I worked all summer, drawing on my recollections. Vague ones; they lacked immediacy, and I no longer knew what to do with them. I was working to no purpose. Of that country I remembered only the delights, precisely what still lured me to it . . . I determined to return to it one last time, with the excuse of delineating each particularity of pleasure.

When, for the sixth time, I embarked for Algeria, the book I was hoping to bring back with me was quite different from the one I offer today. In it, the most serious economic, ethnological, geographical questions were to be raised; there is no doubt that they fascinated me. I took with me notebooks I intended to fill with specific documents, statistics . . .

Are those notebooks here?

Back in Normandy, at least I tried to rework them into a

more coherent whole. But when I reread them, I realized that their ardor was perhaps their sole virtue, and that any embellishment, however modest, would spoil them. I publish them here virtually without changing a single word.

ALGIERS
(FORT-NATIONAL)

Arrival at Algiers
Thursday, October 15

Gruber Tavern. From this warm room where I am taking
dinner, from this too-bright room, you can see, out on the
terrace, parching people who keep wiping their faces; a
sidewalk; a railing; then a gulf of darkness: the sea.

Friday morning

Dreadful night; thick air; sleep, despite my exhaustion,
lacerated by fleas, mosquitoes, bedbugs, and the uninterrupted racket of the shipyards.

In bed at eight, at ten I get up, crazed with thirst; while
there is still time I run out onto the quay and buy ices and
beer.

At six in the morning, I am up, utterly unable to sleep.
Not a breath of air. Scarcely any diminution in heat after
the torpor, the breathlessness of the night.

My room, in the corner of the hotel, opens onto the upper terrace, faces the town, and overlooks the harbor. Above the sea, at the base of the sky, a thick layer of fog, of mist, conceals the sunrise; it looks like clotted heat.

Sirocco blowing. Impossible to breathe. On the terrace, barefoot; the tiles are warm. Everything is leaden; the most delicate white tints are withered. You feel that the sun, once it has risen above this wall of mist, will make the heat overwhelming. And in one bound, the sun rises above it.

The market this morning; no longer in the open air, alas! but roofed over. Brilliant fruits, tomatoes, eggplants, and marvelous tubers the color of clay and of skin which you must nonetheless bring yourself to recognize and name potatoes.

Turkish bath; the same one where, *due anni fa,* Ghéon joined me, furious. How it rained! And then how beautiful it was! But the clients, alas! have changed; now everything seems stale to me; I am no longer young.

Looking for a room, in Mustapha, I visit everything, explore everything. I was thinking, before coming here: any bed, anywhere; and everything seemed possible to me; I am beginning to believe myself no longer possible anywhere.

And these flies!

Then down to the Jardin d'Essai; dash through it; run to the beach . . . ah! to get into the water! . . .

Warm water; deep breaths; peace; languor.

The Jardin d'Essai, in the evening. The bamboo alley already dark . . . I have walked here, evenings, at the hour when you could scarcely distinguish the thick sheath wrapping of lianas from the trunks of the plane trees . . . I go back up to the Gruber, where I write this. I'm going to sleep.

But I shall have seen, so huge! those ipomeas you used to talk about. Twining stalks, violet or lilac flowers which always turn outwards; their cold colors can dazzle! . . .

Giant lantanas; oleanders; hibiscus, ice-green foliage, crimson blossoms. To sleep.

Saturday

Ninety-nine in the shade. It hasn't rained for six months.

The strange, the exhausting thing is that the nights are hotter than the days. For by day, if you have the sun, you have shade, which a breath of air can momentarily refresh. But after six at night, the wind drops; a dark, even heat sets in. Everything is thirsty. You dream of swimming, drinking. You tell yourself: I won't be able to sleep tonight; and you go for a prowl. Even the sky is impure; without working up to a storm, these are the heat blotches which remind you of the vast, scorched continent out there, beyond the propitious Sahel.

I drink; I drink! how I drink!

I sweat; I sweat! how I sweat!

I remember the withered oases . . . There: I'll go there! —oh! stifling and leaden evenings under the palms!

I have not yet been able to find out where that scent of sandalwood comes from, or where it goes, drifting under the branches of the square, enfolding you and filling your nostrils.

An hour before sunset, invisible birds in the fig trees on the square begin a cheeping so shrill that the whole tree is drunk with them.

Saturday, October 17

The harbor activity does not stop for one moment during the night. The balcony of my bedroom overlooks it, and all night long I hear the stevedores' cries, the impact of the bales, the whistles, and above all the unbearable vibration of the winches.

This morning, I shall go looking for pure, cool air up on the mountain; I leave for Tizi-Ouzou at six.

Waking at five, in darkness. The sky, uniformly gray, promises tremendous heat.

The cloud of heat is so low that even from the Jardin d'Essai you lose sight of the upper city.

Here is the golden beach where I went swimming yesterday. Oh, how refreshing the sea would be now! As soon as I am on the beach, the surf runs up, as if the sea were taking a breath . . .

This third-class coach is like a leprosarium. In one corner, a bundle of old clothes; they come apart when the railway employee passes through, and inside you can make out an unimaginably pustular face; the ticket taker does not ask twice. A little later, an Arab vomits.

Fair at Tizi-Ouzou

Torrents of dust on the road. Vendors of little bundles of figs on the edge of the fig groves. Watermelon vendors. Extraordinary animation, unlike any I've ever seen, except in Brittany, on the Sainte-Anne roads the day of the great pilgrimage.

Crowd. They all seem of exactly the same social class. Only Ali and Saïd are handsome; but even their beauty dissolves in the homogeneous mob.

Saïd doubtless recognizes me, but barely shows it. It is in the heart of the marketplace that, guided by Ali, I find him again. Like his brother Ali, he is wearing the huge pointed Kabyle hat over his turban, or over the nape of his neck and falling down to his shoulders. Saïd has grown tall, and he has the most beautiful eyes in the world, harsh features, a cruel and mocking mouth, an oblique glance. His delicate dancer's feet have thickened, spoiled by walking; they should have trodden only lawns or carpets.

Akli, their father, is wearing blue glasses and looks more and more like a bearded vulture, someone certain to rob you. We take tea. I leave Akli with Saïd, and set out again with Ali, who wants to show me their house.

Here we are in a square room, no furniture. A lamb bleats in one corner. On the floor, Ali's wife, a child of sixteen, maybe less, nurses a sickly baby. Ali's mother, in front of the doorway, is nursing her last son. In this close household, these three generations cohabit. Still other children, brothers, sisters, cousins . . . I am offered fried honey-cakes.

On the Fort-National Road

Tiny, heavily laden donkeys, sometimes ridden by an old Arab; they are gray, with thin dry limbs, and crop in passing the fallen acorns, sheep droppings. Tiny gray cows, with the same thin dry limbs . . . The carriage jolts everything; we pass.

Splendid trees; some covered with vines to the very top. The terrain slopes down, but the trees shoot up; nothing supports them in the blue emptiness.

The grapes have been picked. If a single pomegranate still hangs from a branch, I thirst for it!

I have made this long ascent taking shortcuts up the side roads and almost all of it on foot; a fine walk. But I would have liked that mouthful of the wild pomegranate I tore from the tree to be less intolerably acrid. It had split in the heat, and was showing its almost white seeds. There was juice everywhere; but I realized why the Arabs' thirst had rejected it: already, in its wild state, the fruit's scent is revealed, but it takes long cultivation to sweeten, soften, and temper it . . . Yet I persisted, took another bite, and for a long while my gums and lips kept the sensation of an aromatic astringence, a kind of savory contraction.

Fort-National, Sunday

This morning, waking, the same mist as last year. What a relief, after all that sun! I inhale it voluptuously.

You hear, once the nearby noises die down, the cries of that remote village, which I would soon visit. You would think it inhabited by goats. It is perched at the top of a crag, and a single road leads to the houses on the crest; through the openings, your gaze, carrying through the courtyard, plunges into the void. The walls are white-washed; the roofs raisin-colored. The men are ugly, the women extremely beautiful. A whole tribe of children follows me. —How cool the air is this evening! And how good it is to be alive! How enchanting the color of the sky! A visible moisture fills you with delight. Why does everything seem to be smiling? Why does everything this evening seem as happy as I am?

It is not the late season which strips these high trees of their fronds. There is not enough feed for the cattle, and each branch is laid under contribution. And here cows, goats, donkeys, and oxen are grazing on it; the Kabyle's hands are tossing this aerial pasturage down to them.

I remember that slender shepherd, in the gardens of El Kantara, who from the top branches of a tall apricot tree sent down a rain of leaves for his flock. Already tinged by the autumn, the leaves fell as soon as he shook the branches. It was like a shower of gold that for a moment covered the ground, until the hungry goats gobbled them up, one after another.

I'd like to linger another day or two in this countryside; but even if I were to live here thirty years, I could find nothing to say about it; picturesque as any adventure-novelist could wish, it is not to be painted, but describes or tells itself. I may have more ethical pretensions, but as an artist, I am worthless here.

Monday

This morning it is drizzling, actually raining; each Arab wraps himself in a sack. Then the cloud parts under the pressure of overabundant blue. And that street which forms a square, that terrace, that balcony fill with an idyllic and smiling animation.

Acacias line the square, than a steep drop lets you see nothing but the mountain in the distance, opposite us. These idle children are not handsome, but so graceful. There is a gentle breeze, a delectable coolness. The crests of the Djurdjura are in shadow.

Yesterday, after dinner, went out too late; the Arab town was already playing dead. The four or five French cafés, too brightly lit, were indecently perforating the night. I took that suspect stairway which, behind them, leads to the upper city. The Jewish shops are closed; everything is dark; only a skimpy lamp at the top of the stairs. A bench made of two planks; I sit down. And as soon as I do, I hear at the corner of the street the scratchy sound of an Arab guitar. There is a Moorish café here; now I discover its faint glow in the night, scarcely noticeable through the darkness, any more than the discreet sound of the gusla is apparent in the silence. Shall I go in? What will I see but a wretched little stall, twelve Arabs lying around, most likely an ugly musician . . . Let's stay where we are. Let the night penetrate me, insinuate itself with the music . . . An Arab comes out of the café, moves toward me, thinks I am drunk; and indeed I am.

Monday evening

Return to Algiers.

Algiers, Tuesday

How beautiful the weather is now! Not a cloud in the sky. The sea is calm; good time for a journey. The sirocco, suddenly, has fallen, and the temperature with it. It is warm, but less overwhelming. The shade is turning pale blue, the air seems to bear a brightness within it; it is delicious, subtle, almost gay; you could call it *mirth-provoking.* I dream of the oases . . . I'm leaving tomorrow. How lovely it will be, in the evening, the swaying of the fronds! I will no longer think about the past . . .

The indefinable color of these grapes tempted me; I couldn't resist buying some; for three sous, I had a huge bunch. Nothing can express the color of that bunch; it was both violet and golden; it was transparent and seemed opaque; the grapes were not close-set, but covered with a thick bloom, sticky to the fingers, crunchy, explosive, almost hard—so sweet I could eat only four, then gave the rest to the children.

B O U - S A A D A

I

Wednesday, October 21, in the train

I have brought a few books with me; I tried to read, but to no avail. This country enthralls my gaze. It is a latent drama, but if you know how to look at it, one full of anguish, between raw matter and life. There is no longer any question of culture, but simply of existence. Here, everything conduces to death.

Layer of vegetal earth, thin as the edge of one's hand.

Then the terrain, now schistose, cleaves open: it is no longer rock, but really a kind of biscuit. And here, closer and closer together, grow the thirstless pines.

The wind is out of the south; the sky is overcast. Right now it looks like a continuous reflection of the gray schist. No doubt it will be raining soon . . .

Oh, to be a plant, and to know, after torrid months, the rapture of a little water . . .

From the train

Once again, the pines have stopped; the gullied, eroded terrain shelters oleanders in its secret folds. Suddenly a few tufts of a yellow or green pelt, and a few goats to graze on it.

As a salute to the passing train, the little Kabyle shepherd exposes himself, stripping off his gandoura. He seems a goat among his goats, and does not distinguish himself from the flock.

Bordj-Bou-Arreridj

A tiny room, whitewashed walls, and I dread your bedbugs above all! What does the rest matter, your fringed curtains, your broken tiles, your patched bedspread, your stained rug . . . But in the corner opposite the bed, that broken-down divan; a bad sign! And on the marble mantelpiece, those artificial red begonias in clay pots . . . I'm prepared not to get a wink of sleep.

On the shop front of a tiny Arab stall, these words:

LUXE ORDINAIRE

Thursday, October 22

In this splayed embankment of bald, monochrome rocks, the rattletrap carriage jolts down the bed of the wadi. According to the custom of the country, the water flows inland; it will be drowned in the chott.

Detouring the crag, we come on a sudden oasis—not palms but fig trees, tamarinds, almond trees, and oleanders. Then some giant apricot trees, a mill, flocks, some Arabs. And for a long while the oasis stretches out along the wadi, sometimes thrusting itself between its narrowed banks, or, by the extreme aridity of the soil, strangled to being no more, for the bird flying over it, than a green thread; sometimes widening, offering itself, rising until you think: if there's a little sun, its shady places will become suddenly alluring.

But since this morning, the thick, opaque, uniformly gray sky spreads over this golden countryside the tedium of a penetrating drizzle. Not enough water to slake the earth, but enough to muddy it and to dim its colors.

M'Silah

Eight years ago, when I saw the Arabs pray, I took pains not to pass between them and Mecca; I was afraid of breaking the thread.

. . .

O scented gardens of M'Silah! I would have praised you sooner, could I only have known of your existence. The trickling water of your *seguias* tumbled the intoxicated tortoises over each other . . . The frail branch of the pomegranate tree sags with the weight of such heavy fruit . . . A flowering oleander—come closer!

Can it be that eight years have already passed since the evening my friend Athman, in the one tiny garden of Kairouan, taught me that the Arab word for garden is *Dj'nan,* and when it is overgrown: *Boustan.*

. . . It is at this prevesperal hour, when the birds' voices are raised in exaltation, that I want to return there, to be filled with a certain indolence . . .

Approaching Bou-Saada, Friday

Above us, a huge landscape of clouds, which in two hours, at last, we will be passing through.

But the sun, hidden since dawn, still keeps its kind of blinders on. It is long after eight o'clock before it manages to peer through. Its first rays are icy; instead of warming, they chill.

7 o'clock

Before us, those remote cerulean ranges, as we gradually approach, become less blue and seem, drifting less transparently, to be more authentically attached to the earth. And for a long while the questioning eye discerns how blue turns to pink, then from pink to russet, and to reddish-blond.

The endless chott of Hodna, whose muddy reaches fray out . . . Only an occasional tuft of reeds forms a wart here and there. Farther away, a sheet of water, or at least its fallacious appearance.

9 o'clock

Cloud! which this morning, at the sky's rim, rose like a tuft of cotton, is it you, now grown so huge, that like the mists of Elias invades the heavens? Alas, alas, you will bear your abundance elsewhere, without sparing a drop for this earth, and the thirsty plants and beasts will receive from you, toward noon, no more than the charity of a patch of shade.

11 o'clock

Beneath this immoderate light, the mirage now grows larger still. Flowing waters, deep gardens, palaces: before the nonexistent reality, like an impoverished poet, the impotent desert dreams . . .

1 o'clock

For the past two hours, at least, while the horses struggle through the sands, the oasis of Bou-Saada, which we could glimpse from the start of our journey, has hardly seemed to grow any larger at all.

A huge fat Jew from Constantine, who is a buyer here in the South, during the second hour of carriage-travel draws the Lichtenberger Nietzsche out of his suitcase and turning to me (and I am too disconcerted to protest), exclaims: "I myself, Monsieur, I know what it is to die for an idea!"

I I

Letter to Madeleine, Saturday

". . . A tremendous disappointment, to find Bou-Saada on this side, and not beyond the mountains; its desert is to the north; it is simply the interior plain of the Hodna and its quite ordinary chott. Between the *real* desert and myself, I *feel* as much as I see the dense and confused massif that is a prolongation of the El Kantara mountains. The oasis, in a notch of the mountain, thus faces north and broods upon the known . . . Here, no caravans return, and there are no departures for the mortal propositions of the desert. The oasis, determinedly charming like that of El Kantara, lacks that tragic grandeur of so many others which seem to encroach upon death itself.

. . . This morning, up at five, I walked, leaving the oasis, down the gully, irresistibly drawn southward, in spite of everything. The countryside became increasingly rough and harsh; a cold wind was blowing, as unrelenting as the current of a river. The sun remained hidden behind the mountain. And once I had skirted the mountain, the heat, with the sun, became so tremendous that I had no notion of doing anything but getting back. I had already gone quite far, having walked straight ahead for over an hour, and without slackening. I wanted to pick for you these oleanders whose last blossoms were fading, already infrequent, but some of which were still very lovely; I supposed them to have a very delicate peach scent, and was disappointed to find them without any odor at all. The noise I was making as I walked was quite misleading in all this silence; stopping, I heard nothing more than the cheeping of a strange reddish bird that was following me—the same color as the rocks. What would have been the good of going any farther? Yet I wanted to . . . Anguish is only in ourselves; this countryside, on the contrary, is very tranquil; but that question clutches us: is life *before* us, or *behind?* Is this the way our earth was—or what it will become? A chaos of rocks—how lovely beneath the sun!

You must have tasted, have *relished* the desert, to understand what is meant by: culture . . ."

Bou-Saada, Sunday

. . . He answered: "I keep the water." Sitting next to the *seguia,* the child was watching over a little sluice which diverted toward his garden the thread of water he was entitled to until three o'clock.

At three o'clock the child stood up, released the water, then took me into his garden with him. His father opened the gate; we went in. The irrigation over, a pernicious coolness prevailed here. Yet this was where we sat down. His younger brother, whom I did not yet know, offered me figs and dates. —I wish I could have told some stories to that child; his big, diverted eyes were already listening to me say nothing at all. —The juice of the syrupy figs had left my fingers sticky; I wanted to wash them in a pool; but the places under the fig and apricot trees, so scrupulously irrigated, did not offer a shoe's width where you could set foot without breaking a tiny dike or bruising some pot plant. After inflicting dreadful damages I sat down again and stayed there a long time drinking in the shade, enjoying the coolness, without thinking of anything, without saying a word.

Leaving the Ksar, without going down to the wadi, I followed a narrow canal of limpid water which snakes through the gorge, skirting the crag. On one side, my path edged along it, almost invisible against the rock; on the other, down below, flourished an undisrupted grove of oleanders whose topmost branches dipped in the canal, while the lowest ones brushed the wadi. The wadi bed was deep and looked still deeper by evening. In puddles and pools, a scarcely moving water whose course through the stones was lost reflected the linen-gray sky. On the other bank, groves and gardens; and towering above it all, the mountain's harsh flank reddening from moment to moment until it finally became the color of a red-gold pomegranate skin; it looked warm and ready to split open. At its base, the palm trees in the groves were black.

Having cleared in one bound the rocky outcrop in whose shadow I was walking, I suddenly found myself out under the open sky. The sun, long since vanished, left the western sky full of splendor; it was from these reflections that the mountain still glowed before me. Three light clouds, without changing the sky's purity, assumed an ornamental luster . . . This is the hour, I was thinking, when the blue smoke from El Kantara blurs and refines the oasis. Bou-

Saada is not so lovely, but the Ksar now filling with murmurs seems, at this moment, to enter into the night, to be
exalted like the African sparrows in the branches, before
sleep touches them.

I I I

Between Bou-Saada and M'Silah, Monday
Impossible to write this morning; the air is icy. From five
in the morning to eight, swathed in my blankets, I try to
be hermetically sealed. The sky, so impeccable yesterday,
is overcast now, and soon after sunrise takes on the hideous
color of some gray salve.

This morning I feel a tremendous resentment against
this country, and I withdraw from it desperately. I hear
myself humming through Schumann's third symphony,
and the Beethoven sonata in C minor, the one dedicated to
Archduke Rudolf; but the violin part escapes me in places.
Finally, as soon as the temperature permits me to expose
my hands to the air, I take a copy of Virgil out of my bag
and reread the Eclogue to Pollio.*

*Though in my opinion, the least beautiful: it has almost none
of those languorous, liquid, and perfect verses that constitute the
enchantment of the other Eclogues.

None of all this suffices; this morning I wish I could go to the Louvre, and reread some La Fontaine.

Two big Basque fellows are driving—tanned, swarthy, seasoned. This morning I am alone with them in the quite primitive van which serves as the mail wagon. Other travelers are replaced by barrels, bags, crates. In the sand the team is struggling through, the Basques lash the horses less with the whip than with their voices: —"Maquereau, la Carne, Cornard, Bijou, la Flemme, l'Espagnol"—each of them is addressed by a special sound. Michel, even more than his nephew, knows how to exploit the resources of this deafening language; after the second stop, when the uncle takes over reins and whip, our progress is a running fire of gutturals.

Overwhelmed by sleep, my head splitting, I leave the front seat and sliding among the pile of sacks at the very back of the van, I vanish into my black cloak and absent myself.

We have started up six gazelles. Dissolved into the rust of the sands, nothing of their escape is visible except their white tails, vanishing.

I learn, as we talk, that my Basques are from Sétif. So much for that.

· · ·

After a dizzying interval, the vast plain seems to transform itself before your eyes: it becomes a liquid surface intersected by eddies, swollen in patches; the circling ground fills with currents and waves, and your gaze suffers from not being able to perceive even the smallest stable area.

The wind is rising; the sails rattle; a squall. Poor brave vessel—more than five hours to port!

M'Silah

Our northern skies produce no such density of clouds. Over this vast thirst, what a vast weight of water will pour down—to change this thirst into instant intoxication, and this clay plain into a marsh.

Six hours on horseback yesterday; ten hours of this rattletrap van today. Tonight, not the tiniest muscle of my body which doesn't complain. As soon as we arrive, I collapse in the first bed I can find, dead to this world from three to five, after a meal of four eggs. Tomorrow, starting again before dawn, I'll have to ride until dark.

Taking advantage of the last gleams of daylight, I follow the course of this torrential *seguia*, in hopes of finding in it one of those black tortoises which so astonished me when

I saw them from the van last Thursday. But no, nothing; and I suddenly found myself very far away, quite alone in the most shapeless of plains, across which was advancing the most inhuman of nights.

Tuesday

A sudden gust of wind has shifted the storm; a few drops are all that have fallen on the arid Hodna, but the sky remains leaden and stained. This morning, this landscape does not waken a single phrase by which I might praise it. With indifference I stare at the grim crag, the oleander-bordered wadi which so enchanted me before. Pusillanimously, this morning, I left the double coach for a compartment, in order to be able to read more easily. Where in this moth-eaten conveyance, though a little more comfortable than the Saada van—where does this smell of sour milk come from? Is it the shabby traveler who is sharing the compartment with me?

Elsewhere, no doubt quite as well as here, I could be seeing: a cow, in order to drink, thrusting out her drooling muzzle—but in the perfect destitution of these surroundings, I watch more closely, and longer, than I would elsewhere. A child is herding the starveling creature; after it has drunk, it stands in front of the water, stupefied, waiting for the child to lead it away. No hope of green meadows; its hunger will find, till nightfall, only the hollow maize stems scantily offered the poor creature by this poor child.

A L G I E R S (B L I D A)

Algiers, Wednesday, October 28

The sky is mournful; it is raining; but the air is calm. From up here on the terrace, I look out to sea; as far as the sea extends, not one wrinkle. It is from out there that you will come; my gaze invents the way and the ship's wake; if only I could see all the way to Marseilles. May the sea bring you gently! and the movement of the waves be mild—I am dreaming of the days when people said: May a propitious wind swell your sails!

On the Admiralty wall, which immediately whitens and shimmers, a sunbeam falls. But the sky remains heavy with rain. How many clouds over the Atlas range! On a day like this, he indeed seems to be bearing the weight of the heavens.

Those three little boys on this stairway down to the harbor—they are sharing, not a fish, but a fishbone, which they have found God knows where (the God who gives the nestlings their nourishment). There is still a little flesh on it, near the head; this is where they nibble at it—each takes about one mouthful the size of a pea.

A few steps down, an old Arab, two fingers stuck down his throat, is making himself vomit. What horror has he had to eat, that he must throw it up? He is dying of hunger.

. . . Yet out of these various elements a new man is being formed, proud, voluptuous, and strong. He seems to combine elements of the Andalusian, the Basque, the Provençal, the Corsican, the Sicilian, the Calabrian: he is the Algerian. How astonishing it is to hear him speaking French.*

As a young man he is handsome, often exceedingly so; his complexion is not light but olive; his eyes are large, languorous, and in him it is difficult to separate fatigue from sloth—it seems more a sort of amorous lassitude; even as an adult, he keeps his mouth half open, the upper lip raised, the way very young children do.

The cannon salvos exchanged this morning by the French and Russian ships madden the birds in the garden. It is as if a sudden hurricane were whirling them away.

*Moreover, he does so very badly; but he speaks four languages just as well—or badly.

How many there are! They circle above the square, and
when they pass they produce the strident shrieking of a
gale.

The guns stop. On the calmed trees, the flock falls like
a curse.

Lack of the fear of death constitutes the defect of Arab
art. They do not shrink from dying. And it is the horror
of death which generates art. The Greeks, who denied
death to the brink of the grave, owed their art to the effort
of protesting against it. Had the Christian religion succeeded, the certainty of an eternal life would have excluded
art (I am saying: art, not the artist—artists are legion
among the Arabs). Art would have flourished neither in
books nor in the cathedrals, and Francis of Assisi would
perhaps have *thought* his *cantico del sole;* he would not
have written it, having no desire to make anything mortal
permanent.

Friday

Last night, at the theater, Jean Coquelin. More out of
idleness than desire, I go to see him in *Le Bourgeois Gentil-
homme.* He interprets the character as a fatuous imbecile,
quite sure of himself. I suspect that the important feature
of Monsieur Jourdain, for all his transparent self-

importance, is his anxiety—the anxiety of someone whose temperament remains quite different from the role he is assuming; he has a constant fear of not making the right gesture. This is what the actor should show us. I was pondering all this as if I were not in Africa. *Le Dépit amoureux,* which was given as a curtain raiser, though quite badly acted, enchanted me.

Saturday

Dreadful squall. Hail, wind, thunder, lightning . . . "There is far too much racket in there," as Monsieur Jourdain was saying yesterday.

Monday

Lost Russian sailors—lost in the alleyways of Algiers, not knowing a word of French nor Arabic—over and over, when they make signs that they want to be taken somewhere, they are led back to the harbor and their ship. They keep holding out a sheet of paper and a pencil to everyone; a postman passes: "Just write down the address of a brothel for them," I tell him, realizing that yet again they will be taken down to the harbor.

• • •

That stagnant smell of urine, of vomit, and of lukewarm filth floating in the stagnant atmosphere of the Turkish bath . . .

There are days when you wonder if it's the meat that's too tough, or the knife that's too dull. In the end it comes to the same thing: you have no appetite.

Tuesday

I don't know what to call this extension of the breakwater out to the lighthouse, enormous cubes of debris conglutinated by some sort of cement; then, out beyond the lighthouse, at the very end of this artificial promontory, on the last block whitened by the first effort of the enormous waves, a narrow refuge where at nightfall you imagine you are entering into the sea's very heart . . . A red buoy rises and falls, indicating the entrance to the harbor. The sky is stormy; the sea black; the cavernous gaps between the blocks roar with each assault of the waves. Not a breath of air though; the waves are huge, without crests, wide and deeply hollowed. Sometimes they catch in a notch of the rock, and the spindrift spatters me. Ah, if only a wave would come strong enough to carry me off—to be benumbed by the sea's green bile . . . In the distance, street lamps come on, up in the city which the darkness lulls.

Intoxicated, deafened, still dizzy from having watched and listened to the waves too long, wedged in this recess of the jetty where I have managed to get myself soaking wet—here I am approached by T. . . . For over an hour I pretended to listen to him, and I had to agree with whatever it was he was saying all the more, since I scarcely understood a single word.

The huge ship—as it cleared the breakwater, it seemed to yield to the waves, about to capsize. Yes, the last wave, as the ship turned, almost knocked it over, but then, raising it one last time, brought it gloriously into the harbor.

And toward evening, the sea, around l'Agha, turned that strange, Oriental green I used to admire in Malta or in Tunis.

The moon, piercing the clouds with a cluster of beams, ·sails into a free field of blue. The sea grows calmer, or am I deceived?—pacified by the silvery oil of this nocturnal glow.

Wednesday

I shall not go prowling anywhere near the sea; my gaze flees the horror of those clouds a gust of wind drives north. Already ruled by Apollo, the sky exults above the upper city. O laughter of houses! depths of the blue! Up there, once evening comes, I shall climb—yes, to the foot of that pink wall, the one that laughs loudest of all, the highest, and which nothing separates from heaven but that one remote eucalyptus branch, rocked by the wind. But, like the object of our desires, will you look so lovely at close range? Happy branch, whose leaves are washed better today by the light than by yesterday's salt shower.

No; a futile thing. One can see the same place twenty times over—never again anew. You look back, you look more—you see less. Perhaps you understand better . . . but the enchanting astonishment is no longer there.

Thursday

It is going to rain again. The sky is heavy, the air clammy. In such weather I can scarcely write. Odd what shadows the slightest cloud in the sky casts on my thoughts . . .

Walked out of idleness, out of melancholy, following the quay as far as the Saint-Eugène district. A black sky; rain on the sea, driven toward us by the wind. Gods! what have you done to white Algiers? Turned that snowy, light cascade . . . into a night-soil dump! So much snow, here, melts into mud. Over stinking garbage, shanties haunted by a ragged populace. A stagnant puddle where joyless, barefoot children wade. And then, for such horrors are but momentary, the worst of all—the real horror of the ship-yards, the distilleries, the warehouses.

But today this landscape sustains and exalts my melancholy. Evening approaches. Still following the quays, I hear myself murmuring Virgil; I look up and I hear the waves, the spume driven toward me by the wind.

Thursday evening

From this gateway facing the city, from the Admiralty mole, I imagine old Algiers as a few prints still show it to have been, letting her bare feet dangle into the sea. These monumental docks, these warehouses behind which the Fishery Mosque is buried, these hideous wharves, these distilleries, these black ships—my gaze erases them and puts only green and white in their place: —The narrow strip of land which links this part of the breakwater to the city revealed the sea beyond it; where the cliffs stopped, the earth was burgeoning with green. A few houses at the water's edge, but scattered. To reach the sea, a ravine. From the white houses leaning over the edge of this ravine, a path down to the sea . . . I imagine it in the evening and, as it leads to the fountain, I see women following it. The fountain is near the sea where feluccas come and go . . .

Alas, alas! that Algiers whitening in the sea air is no more.

What are these children hunting in this garbage heap, like so many hens? Neither pearls nor millet. The rags which cover them so poorly have covered so many others so often that this debris, these remains, this offal, of which so many others have made use, may yet serve them too.

Up there, once upon a time, in a not very secret street, but in a certain secret turn of the street, was a tiny café . . . I can see it now. —At the back of that café, a few steps down, was a second room, apparently quite narrow and opening onto the café itself; from the place where I was sitting, you couldn't see it all—it continued on a lower level. Sometimes an Arab went down there, coming straight in from the street and not reappearing. I suppose that at the back of the second room a secret stairway led down to further depths . . .

Every day I would wait, hoping to learn something more, to see something more. I would go back there every day. I would go back there at night. I would stretch out on the matting. I would wait, and follow, motionless, the slow disintegration of the hours; toward the day's end there remained a subtle ash of time, bitter to the taste, soft to the touch, in appearance quite like the ash of that hearth, between the little columns, over there, near the mysterious cellar, to the left, where sometimes, shoving aside the ashes, a boy wakens the half-extinguished embers, beneath the accumulation of ashes . . .

Sometimes, accompanying himself on the *guembra,* one of the Arabs sings a song as slow as the hours. The hashish pipe circulates. How stubbornly I watch, in spite of myself, the still shadow over there, the matting over the rear door where I saw the dubious figure disappear downstairs . . .

Three months later, the police had closed the café.

One evening I was handed the pipe, with an inviting gesture . . . And the huge mouthful of smoke I sucked in! It is best to smoke hashish on an empty stomach, apparently; I had just eaten . . . I immediately felt something like a blow on the back of my neck; everything capsized; I closed my eyes, and felt my feet rising above my head, and then the ground gave way, vanishing beneath me . . .

A few seconds later, I was in a sweat, a cold sweat; but of the initially abominable discomfort there already remained almost nothing more than a dizziness I might even call agreeable, the weightless vertigo of someone who cannot tell where he is, floating, floating . . .

Another evening there suddenly appeared, pretending to be drunk, a tall, powerful Arab, eyes flashing, knife drawn.

He kept playing with it, testing its edge . . . It was not one of those little knives a roumi might own, but a huge, powerful cutlass, slender and pointed like its master.

Drunk he may actually have been, to some degree, but nowhere near so drunk as he was pretending to be. Everyone knew him, and everyone spoke to him. Over each head he whirled his blade. Finally my turn came. All the rest has been a game, I said to myself, to prepare for what is going to happen next. Let's be ready for it! . . . But what if I spoil everything by seeming to defend myself . . . And what if I don't defend myself at all—what will happen? Already I could imagine vanishing into those dreadful depths behind the café . . . But I did not flinch; simply holding my big cane firmly in both hands, almost level with my head . . .

And nothing at all occurred. The fake drunkard simply went away. The little café once again became calm, and once again I could stare at the matting that hung over that mysterious rear door.

I I

Blida, Saturday, November 7
So I went to see him in Blida, just as, on the boat from Marseilles to Algiers, I had promised I would. He was in

the infirmary, stricken by a fever during his first days of service.

Under his infantry uniform, he looked pretty bad, and his pale eyes were more disturbing than ever. "I thought it would be different," he began. "If I had known! . . . I'm bored. That's why I got sick; I'm bored."

"But what did you expect, after all?"

"A life that wouldn't be the same thing every day. I don't care about living a long time, you know; I want—oh, you know . . . to live as much as possible in the time I have. Don't you understand that?"

"Oh, well . . ." was what I managed to say.

"Look, you want to do me a big favor? Get me some . . . Bring me a little kef. They say it's really great. I'd like to try that, I really would. But the blacks refuse to bring me any (he called all Arabs blacks). Did you ever try smoking any?"

"No," I answered.

"But you'll bring me some?"

"You'll make yourself really sick."

"No I won't . . . Besides, what if I did? Guys like me, we're not good for much on this earth . . . Yes, I remember what you were saying on the boat. Don't start that again—it bores me. Bring me some kef, please."

"They don't sell it anymore. It's forbidden."

"Oh, you can get it—you'll figure out a way . . ."

"You won't know how to smoke it."

"I'll learn."

And in the Rue des Coulouglis, I ran into Kabisch. Though we hadn't seen each other in over three years, we immediately recognized each other. Ah! those expeditions up the mountain! Monotonous songs in the gardens, whisperings in the Bois Sacré by moonlight, dances in the secret little café! What regrets and what desires will be mingled in my memory of you! . . .

"Kabisch, where can I get some kef?"

Docilely I followed him to three Arab establishments; for it was not enough that he thrust under my cloak the little green package which the first merchant had slipped under his burnoose; in the second shop, we had to make a careful choice of clay pipes; and in the third, reeds. I took some for * * *, and then some for myself.

Selling kef is forbidden—or clandestine now, if you prefer. Since the police have closed all the cafés that smell of kef, claiming to associate the odor of kef with the odor of crime, it is no longer smoked except in secret; and since its penetrating scent betrays it so easily it is actually smoked very little at all. There was a time—how can I put it?—when all Blida was embalmed with its narcotic odor. Nowadays, a man who returns here after a few years' absence is astonished, and asks Blida what has broken its spell. —The Rue des Coulouglis no longer has its perfume.

Blida

In the street of the Ouleds, each woman in her doorway, as though before a niche, smiles and offers herself to the passerby.

But the loveliest thing I saw that evening (in passing, and in the time it takes to blink, while a woman was calling to me) through that open door traversed by my desire in a single bound, was a dark, narrow garden I could barely make out, where the trunk of a cypress tree plunged into a pool I could only guess at—and farther on, lit from behind, closing off a mysterious threshold, a luminous white curtain.

Blida barracks

". . . When I ask where it comes from, they tell me that they don't smell anything, that they don't know what I'm talking about. Now I know perfectly well I'm not imagining that scent . . . There! Do you smell it now? No, it's not from a flower. I'd call that the odor of the earth."

And indeed I could detect, rising, and falling around us,

a heady exhalation, not really a perfume but more like the odor Japanese lacquers give off in the spring.

"Well," he added, embarrassed, "when I smell that, in the evening, it's too much for me . . . I can't control myself. I have to go off into a corner and . . ."

November 10

As long as Blida has not irremediably become the ordinary little provincial garrison town it is stubbornly trying to appear, how lovingly, through each of its decompositions, its compromises, and its corruptions, amid the dreadful routine of its patient banalization, I shall seek—as if for a spangle in muddy water—the vestiges of its defunct enchantments, a few lingering delights of its former loves.

Yesterday evening, I made the rounds of the town's Moorish cafés without managing to hear the gusla played once, however clumsily. This is not the right name for this empty tortoiseshell with its belly of taut skin across which two vibrating strings are stretched: one should say *guembr'* or *gnibri.* What is Blida without its perfumes and without its music? Of its young loves is only debauchery left? —Not one of the *gnibris,* last night, had strings. If the child who led me from café to café had not been

so handsome, I should have wept. Already it sufficed that
he sported the absurd name of Abd'el Kader.*

I was served, in the first café, some of that sharp ginger
tea that seems to have come from a murky and sickly
Orient. I'd like to tell, though I cannot, by what charm the
very destitution of the place beguiled me. No images, no
posters or advertisements on the white walls; nearby, the
vague murmur, the cries from the street of the Ouleds
heard through the wall, made the silence seem all the rarer
and more voluptuous; no seats, just matting; and on the
matting, three young Arabs, lying at full length.

What did this alcove offer them, after all, that they
should prefer here, to the entertainment of other premises,
to the laughter of women, to the dances, precisely the very
absence of all such things . . . a little kef. The pipe went
round, from which each in his turn inhaled only a few
puffs. I dared not risk smoking it, fearing not intoxication
but migraine. Yet I let Abd'el Kader mingle a little kef with
the tobacco in the cigarette I rolled for myself. And perhaps that bit of smoke contributed to the reality of my
well-being. That well-being consisted not of the satisfaction
of desires, but of the disappearance of desire and the
renunciation of everything. The door which opened onto

*The name of the local mountain and the local saint.

the street was closed, and the noises of the outside world vanished. Oh, to linger there . . . Abd'el Kader, leaning toward me, points to the sole ornament on the white wall, hanging in the center—a hideous, shapeless, childishly daubed doll, and says in a whisper: "The Devil." Time trickled by. We left.

In the second café, some revoltingly sweet tea mingled with a flavor of licorice.

In the third café, a very old Arab with glasses was reading a story to a transfixed audience. And for fear of breaking the thread, I refused to go in, but sat on a bench outside the door, in the dark, for a long while . . .

Hammam Righa, November 11

The earth, intoxicated by a shower, dreams a sudden spring. Close to the ground and without leaves appear the white, excessively fragrant dwarf narcissus; the tiny periwinkle-blue stems of what I think are grape hyacinths; the pink stars of delicate lilies rather like our crocuses; all these very tiny, timid, close to the ground, and very sudden. This is all the pity the rain's sweetness can extract from this merciless earth!

. . .

The woods of Hammam Righa reminds me of the woods of the Esterel near Fréjus. Same odoriferous dryness; lavender and burning resins. Same bright, dry, glistening foliage which the autumn neither reddens nor yellows. Same blue sky.

In this enchanting, brilliant, radiant weather, everything, this morning, looks splendid. The blue-tinged air seems new; I feel it filling me with health, with vigor. I shall walk up into the mountains—up there, beyond, with no goal, without a guide, without a path.

Hammam Righa, November 12

It was hot; toward noon I was thirsty, and longed to bathe, not in the dreary pool of the modern establishment, but in the old and almost abandoned Turkish bath still frequented by a few poor Arabs in the lower Hammam. A slope down from the hotel garden leads right to it. The sound of trickling water. The air is soft, shadowy; under vaults of foliage sleeps a refreshing green darkness . . . Here is the old Hammam; near it, a café; on matting, three stupefied Arabs are dozing. I enter through a courtyard where a rooster is crowing. A stairway leads down to the pools.

I push open, noiselessly, the door to the high, vaulted hall. I face a transparent thread of water. It falls from the top of the vault into the middle of the pool, a cascade, and from the whole pool rises once more toward the vault in the form of steam. A narrow rim, all round the pool, makes a frame with which the water lies flush. It is warm . . . No one in the dark hall; a thick mist; but, from the back of the ruined vault, four sunbeams, O wonder! perforating the suffocation in a single leap, squash against the greenish wall.

Blida, Friday, November 13

On this abandoned divan, I shall inhale for a long while still the earthy, vegetal smell which the faun left behind; then, in the morning, wakened at dawn, I shall fling myself into the delicious air.

I I I

Algiers, Saturday, November 14

Hail! morning filled with smiles. All the day's laughter can come—I am ready.

The sea, just touched by the sun, stretches up before me like a wall of light, a pane of iridescent glass which, scarcely distinct, the fine line of the mist-softened, spongy-looking hills frames and separates from the sky. In the still-misty harbor, invaded by the smoke of enormous ships, a scattering of boats seeks the bright open sea, and occasionally, oars extended, seems to soar on the fluid light. And staring up at the sun from the earth, between the bustling quays and the sky, the city laughs.

My eye which, in the absence of sunshine, has been fasting these last ten days, wakens in the sun, wanders, and gazes with appetite.

From the top of the Rue de la Casbah an orange begins rolling and bouncing; a little girl rushes after it; the orange escapes . . . If some French boulevard did not stop them, both would tumble all the way down to the sea.

Sunday, 11 o'clock

There remained, along the wall, no more than a narrow patch of shade which the sun was gradually slicing away; just enough to shelter my thoughts. And of thoughts I already had only just enough left to fill this narrow and shrinking space. Soon, along the wall, there will be only heat and light; and in me only sensation and fervor.

Monday

We had seen, in the market on the square, pomegranates as rosy as these, peppers as green, as purple, sweet onions as glistening, but here, in the sudden recess of the little alley, in the shade, each fruit and vegetable assumed a new luster.

I marvel at the modest profit the Arabs are content with. I dared to bargain for some fruit. Sitting on his heels in the center of the tiny stall, a child was selling them. You might have had the whole stall for a few francs; for a few sous more, the vendor too.

I'd like to be hungry enough, some day, to want to eat some of those chick-peas—a whole handful, which the vendor would take from the top of the barrel and pour into a straw-colored, brine-stained paper cone.

. . . to be thirsty enough to drink from the spigot of the copper urn which that woman, whose face I cannot see, holds on her hip and would tilt toward my warm lips.

. . . to wait for evening, exhausted, in that café, and to be—among those whom the twilight gathers there—no more than one, indistinct, among others.

. . . Oh, to know, when that thick black door opens in front of that Arab, what will welcome him behind it . . .

I should like to be that Arab, I should like what awaits him to await me.

Outside Algiers, Tuesday

You could hear, each time the ramshackle van stopped on the plain, the approach of that shapeless silence which occurs only during very great heat. It fell upon you like a woolen blanket, where a thousand flies were buzzing. You were happy; you were at ease. You were stifling.

It is the aromatic forest that I have chosen this morning—and to breathe its fragrance till evening. O endless expedition! Happy exhaustion of the flesh. —As soon as you leave the secret fold of gully, where the unseen but overheard water trickles, what is still called the forest is no more than a flattened underbrush; bladderwort, mastic trees, and dwarf palms. One slope of the gully held the shade and, despite the great heat, such coolness lingered there that the grass was, as Ronsard would have said, *perleuse*—pearly with dew. In a hollow which a recess in the cliffside concealed, the air was blue and my breath made a vapor upon it. Higher still, among the lavender, I sat down; I pressed the palms of my blazing hands against the icy rock. Before me, on the opposite slope, tyrannized by the sun, everything was scorching. I watched, on the distant crests, white flocks; and sometimes, aided by a breath of wind (so great was the silence all around), I heard a shepherd calling, and sometimes a stronger breeze wrested free a fragment of his flute's melody.

Toward this day's end, I came back to sit on the same cliff once again. Now the sun was baking it on this side, draining the dry grass of its odors. In front of me, on the other slope, advanced the shadow; and when it reached the flocks, these, suddenly moving down, made their way toward the evening's rest.

Algiers, Wednesday

In this crowded restaurant, where you dine worse, probably, than anywhere else—which is no small thing, in Algiers—two Italian mandolin players, throughout the entire meal, pluck and scratch: the air is filled with gaiety and mediocrity.

Restaurant de l'Oasis, Friday

In the middle of the sideboard, on some parsley in a dish, lies an extraordinary monster crustacean. "I have traveled a good deal," says the maître d'hôtel; "I've never seen such things except in Algiers. In Saigon, you know, where you see lobsters as big as . . . (he glances vainly around the room for a term of comparison), such things are unknown. And even here, they're quite rare. This is only the second one I've seen in three years . . . Squillfish, Monsieur . . . *Cigale de mer* . . . It's because of the shape of the head; here, look at it in profile . . . Just like a grasshopper . . . Oh yes, Monsieur, very good; a little like lobster, but much more delicate. Tonight we'll boil it—if Monsieur will come back tomorrow morning, we'll have him taste a piece . . ."

The beast, with six people around it, and all of them discussing it, has nothing to say. It is solemn, motionless, shapeless, blind, the color of mud; it looks like a slimy rock.

"Of course it's alive!" With a touch of his thumb, the maître d'hôtel pokes one of its eyes; the squillfish immediately uncoils its tail with a tremendous force which sends all the parsley on the plate flying; then lies motionless again.

Throughout the entire meal, I watch it.

Saturday

This morning, the beast is still there; enthroned in the midst of the parsley.

"We didn't cook it last night," the maître d'hôtel says; "it was still so alive—I thought it was a pity."

Outside Algiers

I'd have liked this square planted with fig trees to be a little more indolent, enlivened only by the chuckling of a fountain . . . But today the fountain is drowned out by the noisy voices of the vendors; flocks fill the air with dust, and on all four roads of which this square is the intersection, white-clad Arabs hurry toward the market.

Yes, that's the way, I was thinking, that's how the finest roses are produced—only from rosebushes subject to the winter's stupor. On this African earth, so rich and so warm, the tininess of these flowers, which astonishes us at first, their narrowness, the strangulation of their beauty, is the consequence of the fact that the plant never stops blooming. Each blossom opens without energy, without premeditation, without expectation . . .

In the same way, the most admirable human efflorescence requires a previous torpor. The unconscious gestation of great works plunges the artist into a sort of stupor; and not to consent to this process, to fear it, to try to regain control too soon, to be ashamed of one's winters, that is what—in one's greed for more—will strangle and thwart each blossom.

Jardin d'Essai, Tuesday

The noria, turned by a mule, doubtless feeds this square cement cistern, verdant with thick moss. Level with the rim sleeps the water which at first seemed black and which you realized was deep and transparent only when, leaning over the edge, you made out on the bottom a carpet of dark fungosities. An extraordinarily dense shadow, heavy and taciturn, fell from the opaque, icy vault made by a fig tree overhead. Its distant trunk sprouted these branches down toward this moisture. And from the middle of each branch hung a sort of thatch of tiny roots; you sensed *vegetally*, as they approached the water, the effort toward it of all that imminent suction; for as soon as they were in contact with the moist earth or the water, the roots, having achieved their goal, attached themselves, ingested for the famished tree the desired increment of liquid. Then they thickened, formed a stem, then a new trunk; the tree rested the weight of its branches upon it.

I don't know where to place in my sentence this monstrous toad which, flattened on the water's surface, blocked a root cavern, black and grainy as itself; at first I couldn't even make it out: once my cane touched it, a crop of pustules appeared all over its skin. Certainly it ruled over this tranquil basin. Turning it over with my cane, I discerned its yellow belly. It let itself drop down through the water, sideways. Some black fish, quite imperceptible at first, made their escape.

November 27

Three weeks ago, I would have left Algiers more easily; already I have my habits here; little roots . . . a few more days and I shall not be able to tear myself away.

And for so many years already, each year I promise myself not to come back again . . .

But regret for this garden, in the evenings—for this dark garden I visited each evening . . . Ah! how will I endure that?

B I S K R A

November 28, 6 A.M.
Leaving for Constantine

Never have those mountains over Blida seemed so lovely
to me as at that early-morning hour when the sun, still
hidden behind them, did not yet cast a single shadow.
Beneath a shimmering dew, the Mitidja plain flashed every
color of the rainbow; the blue of the sky seemed to be
flowing toward it, emanating from the mountainside. This
wasn't even a mist—it was a blueing of the air; yes, the air
itself was turning blue above the plain, but without losing
its transparency, and seemed all the bluer when the pale
dawn turned blood red over the mountains' crest.

Landscapes seen from the train

The huge fields which, dry last month, I had seen russet
and bare, now turn a brimming green. Barley grows here,

and where the plow has not recently broken the soil, the share enters easily.

So these great bare fields, I was thinking, will soon be covered by deep grass over which the heavy west wind will roll. Each bird, each living atom will swell with sudden joy, spreading its swift wings and singing. Rustles will be heard, murmurs, swift pursuits of love . . . even the insect will not be deceived as to the brevity of such joy: the birth of love and its embrace will be mingled with fever, incipient pleasures will be languorous, and already the flower's scent will suggest the flavor of the fruit.

El Guerrah, Sunday, November 29

The wind! The cold! The sky is clogged with clouds; they look almost motionless, while a great whirlwind sweeps away the dust and smoke closer to us. No tree, for miles and miles, keeps the wind from scraping the ground itself, while the clouds on the contrary, by their accumulation, stand against it, an obstacle: and I imagine, in this absence of vegetation, another cause of these squalls: the sunbeams, encountering no absorbing surface, and all reflecting surfaces being virtually horizontal, develop their heat only when they are just about vertical. And in the same way, nothing retaining it, this suddenly acquired heat can just as suddenly cease. Finally, the air's aridity, or, if the earth has kept some moisture, the rapid evaporation—all this makes the transition from hot to cold almost meteoric.

. . . Everything contributed: the novelty of the place, and of myself, discovering everything with delight; and no tortuous system, so much as my puritanical upbringing, could have prepared me for enjoying so many fresh pleasures. And just then I had the luck to fall ill, quite seriously ill it is true, but of a disease which did not kill me—on the contrary—which weakened me for only a little while, and whose most obvious result was to teach me to savor life's value. Apparently a sickly organism is more porous to the reception of sensations, more transparent, more tender, and of a heightened receptivity. Despite the disease, if not because of it, I was all response and delight. Perhaps the memory of that time is a little blurred here and there, for I have a poor memory in any case, but from the clusters of sensations I brought back from that first journey to Africa rises still a perfume so intense that sometimes, in order to savor the present moment, I am actually thwarted. I forbid myself to make comparisons, however; but I do worse still: six times I have returned to that country, demanding the past from the present, flogging my emotions, requiring of them, still, that freshness they once owed to their novelty, and from year to year finding in my aging desires rewards ever less vivid . . . Nothing compares to the first contact.

Monday

No doubt, ten years ago, the train schedules were not the same, and I am sure that one reached Biskra only by night—for among the vague and painful memories of that endless journey (I was ill), nonetheless this moment comes back to me with extraordinary precision:

After Batna, the sun set; we are coming down to the plains—the air is growing warmer, hour by hour. (The last two days' travel had extinguished me.) A night stop—the air already suffocating. The station has the rather absurdly poetic name—though that first time, it set me dreaming—of Fontaine-des-gazelles. I open the door: extraordinary silence, of a strangely new kind. The air's softness bathes your eyes like a lotion. Nearby, the call of a toad, a single note, pure, bucolic, of which I will be reminded, later on, by the Arab flute. Through all my wearied and blighted senses, I drank in . . .

Such memories are venomous.

To Biskra by train

Under a gray sky, a stretch of gray water; the color of rain, rumpled by the wind's determination; no waves, though, for this water has no depth; at its rim, it is no more than a saliva, a froth; a gray sand mixed with salt extends it, mingles with it, scarcely distinguishable from it; then it is no longer sand nor water; some pasty, intermediary element which, white as salt, assumes a thin magnesian crust. A horse's careless hooves have made muddy holes in it.

I remember that one day, when that salt and that water reflected nothing but the sky's blue, when sky and water seemed to blend in the distance—I saw these margins blooming with pink flamingos. The train passed quite close to them; some flew away, it seemed as if the wind from the train lifted them; then, a few wing-flaps farther on, they idly let themselves drop down again.

Biskra, November 30

I return to the heart of my youth. I step in my own footprints. Here are the delightful margins of that path I used to follow, that first day when, still weak, released from the horror of death, I sobbed, drunk with the mere amazement of *being,* with delight in existing. Ah! to my still-tired eyes, how restful was the shade of the palms! Sweetness of pale shadows, murmur of the groves, perfumes—I recognize it all, trees, things . . . the only unrecognizable thing is myself.

This garden in the hotel courtyard, this garden I saw being planted, is already leafy, overgrown, dense. It is dim under the trees, full of mystery . . .

How good it would be, if there were not so many poor men upon the earth, to speak together here, quietly, with a few friends, this morning.

Beside the mill, so low that a few dwarfish fig trees almost concealed it, we liked to come and sit for a while. Can it be ten years ago? A little gray donkey came here loaded with wheat, and took away the flour. Nearby the tents of nomads whose children we had made friends with, and the dog. Paul Laurens was painting, and little Ahmed would bring us eggs, then sit beside me, not speaking a word.

The river has been diverted from this delightful place; leaving the mill, it used to flow at the foot of this jujube tree which, for lack of water, is now withering away . . . Its shade was so perfect . . . What demon has brought me back here?

Edge of the Oasis, beyond Guedesha
On this side, the desert is shapeless. Toward the horizon, it seems to rise into a bowl. The soil is sandy, ashen; some sort of vegetation, without any verdure, creates, in the distance, the scabby and gritty look of this soil. The sand shimmers in the sun. A kind of persistent mirage blurs the

distances; you cannot properly situate any object—and moreover, there is no object to be seen all the way, to the rim of the sky. To the right, a wing of the Djebel which extends toward Tolga; the crag splits the sand sheath in places; from this distance, it looks like an eczema . . .

Yet I know that when you come closer, this delicate sand is so delightful to the eyes that you can never tire of watching the shadows descend over it, and so inviting to the feet that, having pulled off my shoes, I remember having climbed to the top of the dune barefoot . . . That was ten years ago. I was with Mohammed and Bachir. A snake—harmless, they told me, but terribly long—disappeared like a whiplash, and almost between my feet . . . I remember the person I was . . .

From the top of the highest terrace
Friday

Darkness slowly falls over Biskra. Is it evening, already? Or that dreadful cloud, growing ever thicker? It blankets the sky from one rim to the other. It comes from the abysses of the desert, from beyond Touggourt, from Ouargla, from the deepest heart of Africa; perhaps it is swollen by the mists of the Great Lakes; it is filled with horror and threat; it is yellow. It is not like those of our countries; I want to call it something other than a "cloud."

It drags on the ground, beyond the palms; it hides the mountain from view. It is bright; it is sandy-gray, it is smooth everywhere, like a cloak, only a little brighter at its threadbare zenith. The white walls of the houses turn livid and the pink tiles ashen. I think of the djinns . . .

The sunset gun is fired . . .

Saturday

The haze, like a threadbare cloth, has frayed away at the rim of the horizon. Is it through that blue vent that the wind, this morning, blows with such stubborn insistence? The sand is blinding; one is frozen stiff; against this wind, neither cloak nor burnoose is much protection. The sun, behind the mist, transpicuously silver—flat as a worn medal.

I had planned going for a swim this morning at the melancholy Fontaine-Chaude. But in such weather, crossing the desert—means dying of cold and asphyxiation and horror . . .

Let's go anyway.

Misery and desolation! I sit down sheltered from the wind by a pile of clay, sand, and stones, near the dilapidated rim of a sullen lake, where the water is stagnating among the thick reeds. And if at least some flute-playing shepherd came here, pasturing his skinny goats . . . I am alone. I search myself for some superabundance of being that might, in the contemplation of so much desolation, people all this death with a breath of life. I remain where I am. The wind stirs the reeds. An uncertain sun attempts to smile at the desert, and like a cosmetic on the corpse, silvers the salt crusts.

It would be good to climb this path into the mountains, where nothing but footsteps have made those whitening patches in the rock. You can see them, escaping, rising to the col, then skirting it to go—where? An unbearably cold wind keeps me from making the attempt; returning to the Hammam, I take a simmering bath.

At the cadi's

The little hall opens directly on the street; camels pass by. In a second hall, forming a sort of alcove off the first, in front of a tiny desk, the cadi. He speaks softly, and his handsome face is smiling. In the first hall, which a breast-high screen separates from the alcove, some Arabs are waiting. They are sitting on a broad bench around all four sides of the room, interrupted only by gaps for the door and the alcove; bright-green tiles are set above it; at the foot of the bench, Turkish slippers are piled. The whitewashed ceiling; the walls painted green halfway to the ceiling. In front of me, a fine old man with a long beard and blinking eyes; his poverty preserves a discreet dignity; his body retains only just enough flesh for his soul to dwell in it still. I admire the rich and becoming harmony of his swarthy skin and the sober folds of his turban and burnoose against the green background.

Athman, in front of the screen, speaks to the cadi, explains the very complicated purchase of the house his mother is now living in; on my advice, he wants to make this transaction legal. The cadi listens to him with no sign of boredom, as he might listen to a story; sometimes Si Malek the vendor interrupts; each of them speaks softly. Other Arabs come in, begin waiting on the bench. A tireless patience is in the air. Against the door, a one-eyed child sings a religious litany; a pious Arab hands him a coin. Camels pass.

Jardin Landon

Yes, this garden is a wonderful place, I know—and yet it does not really delight me. I am trying to discover why. Perhaps, because of the very care with which it is kept (in the sandy lanes, not a leaf underfoot); nothing seems natural to me here. It is a work of art, you will say. Granted; yet this lack of abandon, of indolence, would not delight me in any enterprise. Besides I populate a garden, immediately, despite myself, with figures in its own style, whose gestures and sentiments form a certain harmony with it. Thus I saw at the Villa Pamphili the low bows of a Van Orley in seigneurial robes, and Dante and Beatrice in the orchards of El Kantara. Nothing exceptional in my selection; I see Goethe at Dornburg, composing his *Iphigenia* there; Tasso at Este, between the two Eleonoras . . . Here I cannot help seeing the characters of Jules Verne; they smoke their Havanas; they speak of dollars, not francs; they have not read our Racine; they are always leaving tomorrow . . . It is true that I also see Gautier's *Fortunio* here, or Stevenson, which is no hardship. And I also see characters out of Gauguin; what surrounds me here is their flora, artificially acclimated; bamboos, coconut palms, monster ficus . . . By an ineluctable suggestion, the merest palm tree, once it reaches full leaf, suggests some *other* country where such vegetation would be still more natural.

What a sophist you are, Maurras; there is no question of severing one's roots—*"déraciné"* has never implied that. The admirable thing, precisely, is that the English, like the Romans, have been able to take their roots with them, wherever they go.

In Lady W***'s room, you no longer feel you are in a hotel. On her travels she takes with her portraits of her

family and friends, a tablecloth, vases for the mantel
. . . and in this ordinary room, she lives *her* life, at ease,
making each object around her part of herself. But most
surprising of all, she has been able to make a society for
herself as well.

We were four French households, each conducted apart
from the rest, each discreet, polite, but living in the hotel
as though in disgrace. The English—there were twelve of
them—without having known each other previously,
seemed people who, having expected to meet each other,
had finally done so: comfortably informal in the morning,
smoking pipes and attending to various tasks; in the evening, in patent-leather slippers, in evening dress, proper
gentlemen. The conquest of the hotel salon was easy for
them; it would have been futile and indeed presumptuous
to attempt to dispute their claim to it, so normal did it seem
for them to hold forth there; they knew how to make use
of the place, we did not.

And moreover, as I said, they formed a society; we did
not.

I have never met any but two kinds of French people
traveling (and most of the time I have not met any at all);
the *interesting ones,* who isolate themselves and always
communicate the feeling that *they are not at home;* and the
others, who noisily form their chattering, banal, repugnant
groups. And are the English repugnant? Certainly not! On

the contrary, very attractive; those three young artists especially, a little group apart within the group itself; painters?
literary men? whatever they were, reading their Stevenson
and their George Moore, I would have been delighted to
talk to them, if only I didn't get such stage fright at the
mere thought of doing so in their language. Besides, what
would we have said to each other? Then, I feel so inferior
compared to them, and if, as an individual, sufficiently
aware of his worth, I have quite enough pride not to mind
that at all, as a Frenchman, it is intolerably painful.

I suppose I must set down here one of my mortifying
recollections: I was traveling with P. G.; it was evening; our
train would not arrive till dawn; we were wondering how
best to accommodate ourselves for the night, and on this
account, fearing the increase in the number of travelers, we
had, with our bags, our cloaks, our blankets, probably
taken up more room than was necessary. Occupying two
rear corners, two Englishwomen watched us without a
word. Another Englishman appeared, looking for an empty
seat, took only one, and settled down. The train started.
And then this happened: slowly, irresistibly, the two
women and the Englishman expanded and finally it was
they who took up the space initially earmarked for us; and
we could do nothing about it; at first because we didn't
really need all that space; and then because it would have
seemed to us indecorous, as Frenchmen, to spread our-

selves out, thereby preventing those two women from doing the same. We knew very little English; having realized this, our travelers took advantage of the situation to speak about us. We knew enough to understand that the man was saying to the women:

"Amazing, these French! They always begin by taking up much more room than they need. But they don't know how to keep it . . ." Then he added, with a laugh, "And it's the English who get the upper hand."

This was the beginning of a conversation whose echoes kept us awake far into the night.

Tonight, on the terrace cantilevered over the darkness, at the very edge, we watch the moonrise. A sort of dawn, a pallor above the mountains precedes it. In this place, the mountains seem to swell gently. Is it a cloud that extends them? Yes, opacity inflates, then, as though under pressure, explodes, tears, and forms a crater through which, pushing back the notched edges, appears the moon, breaking free. Full tonight—full as an egg. Another instant and it will be completely laid. It is still swelling. How big it is! Already it could no longer fit back in the dark crater. How round it is! What would you say if, suddenly, with a single leap wrenching itself from the ground, you saw it rushing to the top of the sky and exploding—or rolling toward us down the slope of the mountains across the plain?

Sunday

Splendid weather. For days now, I had scarcely been alive. This morning, through my shutters, I felt the sun rising, radiant. I went out into the icy air. Everything was being born . . . Nothing is so beautiful as this matinal felicity. My joy, in the course of the day, does not grow from hour to hour; I feel it is already complete and total upon waking—all the more alive since the day to be filled with it will be that much longer—since I have got up that much earlier.

Near the hotel, the gate of the friendly square is open. I go in; I sit down on the bench. Frej', who is married to the lovely Jewess Goumarr'ha, is sweeping the walks, trimming the garden. In front of me, in the plant-clogged pool, the water drips on a mossy rock, making a lapping sound. I write these lines.

No, the sky is still milky, almost white; it must be perfect, if my exaltation is to be perfect too.

Sidi Taïeb is a marabout. His virtues protect the town. As he is often to be seen with prostitutes, and since he seems to be having such a good time, I have tried to make Athman explain what his virtues consist of; but on this point Athman brooks no joking; and though I try not to smile, my mere question suggests a doubt . . . Sidi Taïeb is an article of faith.

Sidi Taïeb enjoys the greatest consideration; this is expressed by gifts. Sidi Taïeb is severe; he scorns money; he prefers garments. The pious, who among us would have a mass said, buy a burnoose for Sidi Taïeb.

Now even though he has so many of them, Sidi Taïeb never changes his burnoose. As soon as the one he has on is dirty, he pulls another on over it. He is wearing about twenty, one on top of the other. You can't imagine how he could be any bulkier.

Certain fine evenings—Athman tells me—in front of a big fire, on the square, stripping off all these burnooses, Sidi Taïeb appears stark naked. It is apparently when the lice become too much for him. A few pious disciples, extracting the inner burnooses, throw the three or four oldest ones into the flames, where the lice die, with a crackling noise. Then Sidi Taïeb dresses himself again, and new burnooses, for his delight, rain from heaven.

Under their weight, he cannot walk; he rolls. One day I saw him coming toward me: he looked just like Ubu setting out for war. Another day, supported by two whores whom he was doubtless sanctifying, two Ouleds in festive array, and following the exalted procession moving with music and great racket toward the tomb of Sidi Sarzour, he was laughing, staggering, stumbling; like some drunken Silenus.

Fine as he was in this fashion, I prefer him motionless. Kneeling, sitting, crouching . . . who knows? All you can see is a round mass dandling this way and that. He stays that way far into the night; in the center of the Square, he looks like the Holy Ampulla; he has the precise shape of a nipple.

A staircase, and at the top a prostitute's lodgings, now replaces the shadowy café in the street of the Ouleds where that first year I would go to forget time, evening after evening.

These two streets of pleasure lie parallel, so close that at this point more than one café opens onto both at once— these two streets, which communicate with each other by three cross streets, are not, as so often happens, in a forgotten corner of the town, of difficult and clandestine access; no, they open quite shamelessly onto the most ordinary, the most central space, near the market. A public garden opens off them; the air here is not the least foul-smelling; it is air from open spaces which passes through the scented garden. If everything debauched and suspect in the town is to be found here, so is everything noble and agreeable. Here everything brushes up against everything else without the least ill will; the poorest mingle with the rich; the young with the old . . . everything is mixed together. The timidest child passes close to these whores without turning his eyes away; the wisest old man as well.

In a slightly recessed café, protected from the noises of the street, the same Arab to whom I listened last year is reading ʿAntar still. A few benches at the entrance; on the floor, matting. Here, a white-clad crowd is lying and listening. Among so much gentle whiteness, nothing stands out, everything dissolves, melts away; the shaded light envelops everything without incident; it seems a soft, slow-flowing liquid, without reflection, without laceration. The man reading ʿAntar aloud is very handsome; his voice assumes triumphant resonances. Sometimes, looking up from the book lit by a candle, he explains and comments on a verse. When he reads, he punctuates the verse with one hand; the other, close to the candle, holds the book. Sometimes a laugh shakes the crowd, rather like the one, I suppose, which shook the table of the gods on Mount Olympus; it is one of ʿAntar's witticisms, some brilliant Arab exploit. Captives, defeated, the listeners find a solace, a respite, and a certain aliment of splendor in the narrative of their ancient prowess . . . The reader marshals the words; his voice rolls like a drum; one hears nothing of the verse but its heroic sonorities. How beautiful they were, and how victorious!

. . .

Leaving the crowd and my shadowy companions one
evening, I go with Athman and sit down in front of that
smaller café, in the place we call: *the terrace*—which is here
only a wooden bench and a dark table. Here Sidi M. joins
us; he is an Arab from Touggourt, well-dressed, talkative,
his beard carefully barbered. He knows the desert from the
borders of Morocco to those of Tripolitania. He talks of
In-Salah, of the Touaregs. His voice is musical; he pro-
nounces each word so clearly that sometimes I imagine I
can understand him. Athman translates.

Sidi M. is a wise man; which is to say, apropos of
everything and anything, he cites a text; the older the text,
the more it is venerated. He believes in every Arab fable;
he will hear nothing of the roumis.

All the learned men I have met in Algeria are the same;
and when Athman "takes instruction" I know what that
means: instead of formulating questions, indiscriminately
collecting a whole tradition of answers. And this is enough
to fill such "scholars" with self-importance. What was
called science, in the Middle Ages, was just this.

"Have you read," Athman asks me, "the story of the
learned Princess in the *Thousand and One Nights?* Now
that is knowledge, that is wisdom!"

When I questioned Sidi M. about relations between
Arabs and Tuaregs: "The Tuaregs," he said, through Athman, "have no use for the Arabs, and frequently attack

them; the Arabs are very much afraid of them."

"But all the same, you see them in the cities of the Souf?"

"They recognize," he answered, "the marabout of Amich, because he worked a miracle against them. All alone, on his mare, he went out against the Tuaregs riding on eighty dromedaries. The Tuaregs shot at him, but the arrows, you see, when they touched his mare, turned soft at the tip and fell to the ground, every one. He himself would do nothing to the men, but with a single arrow he killed sixty-five dromedaries."

He also said: "Out there, the Tuaregs know a country, in the mountains, big, so big, that you can walk straight ahead for ten days; to get there, only one way leads in, and only one man at a time can take it. After all the men have gone in there, the last one rolls a big stone over the way . . . a stone big as this table here, and then no one can see where the road goes. That is why they're not afraid of the French. —A Tuareg told me this in In-Salah."

A few leaves are still dangling from the stripped fig trees; broad, flat, dull gold. Under the palms, in the dry shadows, they drift; they seem to float, until the day when, for his herd, some shepherd, more potent than the winter, entirely strips the branches.

· · ·

And when I shall have described the scent, the whiteness, what will be left to me of this night I would have liked to prolong till dawn? —A dented moon glistened high in the sky. The night before, still full, the moon did not seem so lovely; it had rained; in front of the houses of pleasure you saw only a few Arabs, those who to climb back up to their old villages did not mind the filthy streets and the washed-out paths. On this soft and voluptuous night, there remained only enough water on the ground to soften it, and to form in the air, instead of the usual dust, the bluish mist which blurs each object. And in this nocturnal atmosphere, an harmonious populace circulated.

Here among so many vague whitenesses, among so many shadows, a shadow myself, drunk without having drunk, a lover with no beloved, I walked, sometimes caressed by the moon, sometimes by the shadows, my tear-filled eyes hidden from the light, and exulting in the night, and longing to vanish into it. And sometimes, by a chance encounter, walking with Athman, sometimes with Ali, savoring the moonlight with them like a sherbet, alternately saddened and delighted by all the grace and childishness, despite approaching manhood, their unpolished minds retained.

To recognize these women by their voices; to smile or stop at their call; and in the sudden brilliance lavished by the noise and light of the cafés, to see so much prowling mystery stop, so many shadows for a moment become incarnate, hesitating, then plunging back and dissolving into the night, where I longed to vanish with them.

Ah! had the night been more sonorous still, the air more vaporous, the odors more amorous, what would be left of it all this morning but a shard of ashen memory which I gather up in the hollow of my heart and which a breath of wind will scatter, leaving only a scab in its place.

. . . Here, farther along the empty road, there is a pile of stones to sit on. At sunset each evening, I shall come here. I shall come alone . . . Farther to the right are the nascent dunes; opposite me, the desert. This road leads to Tolga; it is out there, in front of me, that the sky above Tolga catches fire. On the dune the sand, glowing at first, turns to ash. In the heart of the desert, a marsh becomes a puddle of blood. The oasis stretches darkly to my left. From the ground rises a vapor which trembles and turns the gardens blue. No languor here, no melancholy; a burst of inhuman peace, of scattered glory and indifferent splendor. Serene, indifferent, the night rises. Infinitely far away, some nomads light their fires.

If the days are uncertain, the nights are lovely—lovelier than their memory. How can I go indoors, how can I go to sleep, knowing that outside, in the soft air, this bright glow continues, and knowing that the moon, before I leave these places, will illuminate the town for me only a little later each night, and each night only a little more faintly.

Oumach Springs

Here, reeds whitened in the sun; oleanders grew so thickly that when you walked through them, you forgot the desert; this place formed, enveloping, hiding the springs, an almost mysterious retreat which you knew was haunted by hyenas at night. In a fold of the ground, the hot springs spurted up; then, downstream, in a less sheltered place, the washerwomen occasionally took up their work. The sulfurous water, turning its bed green, seemed to run deeper. The sun rose overhead.

Last year, some nomads set the brush on fire; this secret place of the desert they razed according to the Arab fashion; under a fault in the terrain where nothing now protects the place, the mystery of the spring is exposed; the water bubbles up now, shamelessly, in the sun.

The washerwomen have fled. We met, this morning, only a few haggard nomads; near the spring, a dead donkey; and by night, we realized a hyena or jackal would come, to finish tearing off the flesh, running across the desert sniffing the air corrupted by the carrion.

Sunday

No, I shall not waste this splendid day on work! I shall stay outside till nightfall. Radiant weather . . . I address my devotions this morning to the Saharan Apollo, whom I see before me, with his golden hair, his black limbs, his porcelain eyes. This morning my joy is perfect.

During the day's fast, waiting for nightfall, my friend the pauper Bachir plucks the tiny leaves of kef he will smoke in the evening. Thus in the wretchedness of his life he waits for the night of the tomb, and prepares his paradise.

When I speak to him of his poverty:

"What would you have me do, Monsieur Gide," he answers, "it will pass." By which he does not mean that he ever hopes to become rich, no, but that what will pass is his life.

The rest is already enveloped by night; but on this side of the West, an inflammation still remains; through each cross street, in the depths of the desert, you see it. Here a redness lingers where the last fervor of the sun's rays is eroded, and here, touching the dune, level with the ground, far away, a deeper crimson line, a streaming, bleeding cloud, a kind of wound in the sky. Ah! with what abundance of gold, above the dune, the already vanished sun sometimes flooded the plain! What mist now rises! Under its delicate cerulean, the oasis gradually recedes.

Fontaine Chaude

What am I still seeking here? Perhaps, the way a scorching body finds delight in plunging naked into cold water, my mind, stripped of everything, steeps its fervor in the icy desert.

The stones on the ground are beautiful. The salt glistens. Above death floats a dream.

I picked up one of these stones, a pebble, in my hand; but as soon as it leaves the earth, it loses its luster, its beauty.

Tiny four-holed flute, through which all the ennui of the desert is told, I compare you to this country, and stay listening to you divulge yourself in the evening air, ceaselessly. Ah! of how few elements is our noise and our silence made in this place! The tiniest modification is evident. Water, sky, earth, and palms . . . I marvel, light instrument, at what subtle diversity I taste in your monotony, as the boy musician with his supple fingers insists, hurrying your course, or delays it under his breath.

If only from page to page, evoking four shifting tones,

the sentences I am writing here might be for you what that flute was for me, what the desert was for me—of diverse monotony.

Droh

At the edge of the groves, with no outlet, the water stagnates and in a natural ditch protects this side of the oasis. For a long time before entering, it seems that the road besieges it; it lingers around the edges; it seeks a way in. It also seems to hesitate, repelled by the disappointing oasis. The approach to astonishing Droh is dreadful. The ground, beneath the palms, is hideous, it looks spongy the way it was in places at M'Reyer, near the chott . . . Yes, indeed, you hesitate to go in; the road turns again, passes beyond, then at last, near the low mountain, takes advantage of an outburst where the oasis, emerging from its marshes, is choked off between two walls of rocks. Here is the gate to the village.

Oh, I recognize it, step by step. I savor again, harshly, deliciously, its ugliness. The same half-naked bodies, at the foot of the same walls, stretching out . . . And so Droh did not cease to exist! When I leave it, it will continue to exist as well! Did I have to come back here and touch all this, in order to believe in it? What need have I, and to assure what joy, of this desolation without appeal? Yes, you know henceforth that it is here, that it exists. What more to desire now! What more to expect! On your way! —Not yet . . .

Somewhere in this desolate oasis there is a murky place; it is there I would go. There every path disappears; your feet sink in as soon as they no longer stand on the tufa; but a few steps farther, the rotten earth, I know, will let reeds spring up . . . Here they are! This is the moment when the sun silvers them most delicately. In order to bend their shafts, it is enough for a bird to come and perch on them. Out of a complex tangle of oleanders, they leap up, very high; their rockets glisten in the blue air.

I wanted to pick a few of them; but as soon as they were in my hand, they were no more than a bundle of rough sticks tufted with a little gray hemp—utterly without beauty.

. . . And in this oasis where I wander still—for I tell myself I shall never return—on this side are the fresh-water springs; the water runs and sings at the foot of this palm tree; it slakes a vine beside it which coils around the bole of the palm; which sinuously garlands it; then with a leap it reaches the treetop and vanishes among the fronds, leaps out, spreads, divides, then falls back all down one side in an ornament of broad leaves which the late autumn has gilded. The sun plays through them. No, even heavy with ripe grapes, your profusion, eager vine, would not have seemed so beautiful! —Or did it require this environing disenchantment, to give such an accent of splendor to your unexpected gold? . . . Another—still another! I had not seen them last year. Ah! shall I long to return?

Sunday

The fast ended tonight. The exhausted people are ready to fling off their melancholy this morning; but it is raining. This day was to be joyous; it is lugubrious. We have climbed up to the ruins of the old fort where prayers are said in the open air.

A thick mud clings to our soles; the Arabs' piety hesitates—will they kneel here, on the sopping earth, even so?

Some make for the nearby mosque; we go there with them. Toward nine o'clock, the sky clears a little and the prayers are announced. We climb back up to the old fort. Here, almost a hundred and fifty Arabs have managed to perform their devotions on mats. To their left, on a simple earthen seat, a very old priest climbs up too, helped by the others. After a few invocations which the people repeat in chorus, he begins a kind of semiliturgical preaching which he chants in a splendid voice, prophetic and wearied. Toward the end of this predication, the rain begins once again.

We onlookers remained at a respectful distance on the

right—from these I stepped even a few feet farther back, in order to conceal my tears from them. In the piety of this conquered people, which the grim sky seemed not to receive; in this despairing trust in something beyond, in this appeal, rises the desolation of the desert.

"He is telling them sad words," Athman answers, when my companion questions him.

Three times over this strung-out crowd, as though under a wind of prayer, bends toward Mecca, touching the ground with its forehead.

Opposite them, about twenty yards from the preacher, upon a knoll, some tourists, men and women, as well as a group of White Sisters, are training their cameras on the service, giggling and parodying the holy man's voice. They worship another God, and feel very superior.

I have dreamed that I came back here—in twenty years. I passed by, and was no longer recognized by anyone; the unknown children did not smile at me; and I dared not ask what had become of those I had known, whom I feared to recognize in these bent men exhausted by life.

So few are the elements of the harmony that the slightest alteration remains generally unperceived in itself, for a man whose mind resists the spirit of analysis and who plucks his joy stemless; but he is astonished, passing again through these same places, no longer to savor the same pleasures, and, able only to discern the diminution of their charm, blames himself, grows old. It was late before I understood how much, in the streets of Blida, the aromatic smoke of kef was indispensable to my intoxication; in the same way I realize only this morning that here, in the paths of the oasis, an alien substance has appeared; under the compact clay of the paths, a kind of powdery yellow lime shows up. The rain of the last few days, then the steps of the passersby, have spread the clay in lumps, and in places this dreadful substance comes to light; slowly it mingles with the clay, spoils its color, alloys its density, corrupts it, dirties it. That is why, in these paths I used to love, the mud no longer seemed to me so lovely; the clay, after the rain, is no longer so soft underfoot; dry, it is no longer so pink, nor covered, once the sun has dried it, with that delicate crackle.

December 21

Yesterday, an Arab feast day; the rain hardly stopped all day long. The look of the ground in the streets is such that you give up trying to cross them; if you move about, you hug the walls. On the mountaintops, the water falls as snow and lays an abstract whiteness on the russet land. Athman walks, splashing me.

"Someone," he tells me, "paid me a fine compliment today. He told me: 'Athman my boy, you don't know who you are; you don't know what you're worth.' "

How far away are the days when a fine belt sufficed his vanity?

Monday

Babou, the Jewish cabaret keeper, has a sister, and today she is getting married. Three nights in a row, according to the custom, there will be feasting. Open to all. The first night is for the Ouleds; the second for the relatives and for respectable women; the third for anyone. It is on this third night that I came there, out of curiosity; even more, because I had nothing better to do.

The cabaret is a very poor one, ugly outside and cold; the first room I came into was dark, but this was not where the feast was . . .

Now we are in the private apartments. Beside me is a Jew in French clothes, murmuring, smiling, vile. A little farther on, against the wall too, the rather lovely young bride; beside her a dim creature, extremely ugly, with a confused expression, lost in sleep or drunkenness: the groom.

A woman is dancing; the shrill flute of Bou-Azis fills my head with its ferment. Everyone pretends to be having a good time. Obliged by the cabaret keeper, Athman and I take green mint tea; not knowing where to put my glass, I drink it off, but as soon as he sees it is empty, the man fills it again; the last ones I empty out onto the carpet. We leave. It is raining. Leaving Athman, leaving them all, I let the night wash me for a long time.

Tuesday

Was it, after my intoxication yesterday, some lucky indolence of the mind? . . . I made my way into this orchard like Aladdin into the garden of jewels; I walked, staggering, drunk all over again with ecstasy and delight, letting the stammering alternation of sun and shadow play within me. Not a sound, not a song, which was not of some bird. Doubtless at sunrise this garden is steeped in mist, I thought, for there remained everywhere something moist, something touching. At first the morning had been splendid; but—and without the least breeze rising, the sky soon grew overcast. Each object lost its luster, its weight, its reality. I walked on, but in a dream. It seemed to me I was not seeing but remembering, or rather: I was advancing, not doubting that these were real things around me but rather that it was I who was seeing them—so intimately was I identifying myself with them.

Oumach

... The wind rose toward evening. It was painful for our horses to go any farther, and in the sand where the wagon wheels sank in, our footsteps immediately vanished. How lovely that sand was! Raised by the wheels, it fell back in a blond mane; the wheels, as they turned through it, creaked silkily ...

At Sidi Okba, I bought for ten sous the little five-holed reed flute I have here. In the box, there were several of them, each with red designs. The one I bought was the smallest, with the simplest designs. I did not really choose it; of all of them, it was the only one I liked; the moment I saw it I wanted it desperately.

It was well shaped; but when I tried to play on it, out of its clumsily drilled holes emerged only discordant sounds.

Sunday

The sky is clear, but the wind is icy; I need more warmth than this to bloom.

We picked, on the rocky slopes, these tiny, odorless, colorless flowers, which have no delicacy whatever. Even their corolla is ligneous; it closes against the sun. Without a stem, growing right on the ground, they look like conical wooden nails; patellas of rock. Yes, the tap root is immediately succeeded by the flower. It lies there, expectant, scarcely distinct from the dry sand; then, at the slightest shower, it opens and seems rotten.

The distended void of the desert teaches the love of detail.

I have sought the shelter of a garden to write in; an icy wind is blowing, and you can't help shivering, anywhere, in the open air.

We have decided to leave tomorrow morning. Will I be able to? Sometimes, and quite suddenly, a crumb of pleasure wakens an aftertaste so secret that I immediately feel I lack the courage to tear myself away from here.

Sunday evening

In the little garden, which cannot be seen from the road, where you enter by walking through the café—in this little garden we sat down. Afternoon was slowly turning to evening.

Here there was a tiny stream flowing; here a few flowers were fading.

Two slender jujube trees, on either side of us, formed a frame for the trembling expanse of the sky where the sun was bleeding to death. Here Bou-Azis came to join me;

here, like a song of some twilight bird, the song of his flute
filled the air. It was not the faint whistle I was used to
hearing in these places; but bright, shrill, tense, lacerating
the evening and sometimes almost painful. Athman joined
him in a kind of duet.

At each verse that Athman sang, the flute responded,
resuming the melody and turning it a little. To the tune of:

My youth has trickled away in exile

he sang his first poem, and the second to:

I knocked at the garden gate
The nightingale bade me enter;
To me the rose opened the door
and I was greeted by jasmine.

The last to:

I fasted longer than a month
for a single kiss from your mouth.

The moon, still a sliver, was rising through the watery
sky; it gleamed very faintly on Bou-Azis's handsome face;
I admired his agile fingers on the flute that was as dark as
the night.

Monday evening

You will never see again, I told myself, soaking my hands in it, you will never see again, though it is here, this spring, this fountain, where you come to sit in the evenings.

Here flows an almost silent water, which my hands entered without a sound.

I hear, around me, the errant noises of things . . . I remember . . . I came here one evening by moonlight. Palm trees, in the blue glow, curved down to the water like shadows . . .

No, never again, never, I shall remind myself, this calm water—yet it is here, here still . . .

T H E   R E T U R N

Tunis, December 28

In vain we searched, on the hill of the Belvedere, for those dwarf iris, their blue so gently tinged with violet, which, yesterday, between Constantine and Tunis, bordered so much of the road in such profusion. If only we could have picked them—I would have liked, in my Normandy garden, to have tried to acclimatize a rhizome, as I did that strange onion I brought back from the C***, but which, for two years, persists in sprouting only leaves.

Lake of Tunis

Polders . . . which owe their beauty only to the light.

It has always been this way: the most uncertain terrain allures me.

I arrived near the harbor. Two Italians took me out in their boat. Slowly, deliberately, we drifted among the hulls of the great ships. We ducked under the cables. There was only the faintest breeze; the water of the lake was shallow; the ground, here and there, thrust up through it. For a moment our boat stuck in the mud, and from the effort of the oars rose a fetid smell. Stakes, occasional or in rows, indicated certain points of outcrop, I imagine; they were not much different from those marking the oyster beds in Brittany, in the vicinity of Locmariaquer . . . I immediately recalled those sea-green places, and the boat I was in became the one where once, more slowly, more deliberately, and with even more pleasure, I drifted one evening between the low islands of the Morbihan. That was summer; the air was warm and the water of the sea tepid; after the sun had set, without mooring, we swam. The sea was shallow there, and the colors of the deep interrupted the squamous reflections of the sky . . .

Messina, January 3

An uninterrupted rain dims the coast of Calabria, which fades out and occasionally vanishes entirely; then all you see in the vast window recess above the stone balcony moss-green from the reflection of the low shutter—all you see are the masts of two boats . . . I don't know why I'm writing this.

Naples

From the hotel dining room, brightly lit and likely to seem almost luxurious when you have a few glasses of Falernian inside you, you hear through the curtains, through the open window, the traditional serenades. How indecently affirmative and direct such music would seem to an Arab! Everything vulgar in the Italian soul, everything declamatory and voluptuously sentimental is exaggerated in the facile tune. Even so, it attacks a weak spot, and once spring is added, I am easily snared.

Naples

Between two mechanical pianos, I read, I ruminate, and stare at the sea. Ah, how easily the gentle dazzle of Italian splendor becomes natural to me. I marvel how readily I feel as if I were no longer traveling. I recall the "little habits" Nietzsche advises, those the studious exile constructs so industriously for himself for a few days, a few weeks, or a few months, the ones which protect him against boredom and sustain his work; the ones which so delight the assiduous mind, as soon as, released from worldly obligations and those of society, it accepts constraint only from itself, yet imposes one upon itself, and a severe one, but always with a view to work, so that the strictest is also the preferred variety. Born of the sense of exile, there subsists throughout the work a kind of constant vigil, a heedless exaltation, by which the mind remains attentive, ready for effort, apt for the boldest understandings, and not losing for an instant the feeling of the moment's worth.

I am not saying this *against* Barrès, but I am thinking it *in spite of* him.

Rome, from the Monte Pincio
Late January

These roofs are beautiful. The setting sun, hidden by a narrow cloud for a moment, nonetheless illuminates them. It has been raining; from the depths of the streets a mist rises; from the Janiculum, a mist rolls down. Leaning over the balustrade, clinging like Polyhymnia in the posture which makes a passerby say "there's a dreamer," I am not dreaming at all; I am looking. The flat roofs, iced by the shower, glisten. In the moist evening air, the chaos of houses dissolves; the streets look like streams; the squares like lakes. And rising into the light, domes and campaniles . . . No, I am not dreaming. And what would I be dreaming about? Why, facing this *reality,* would I close my eyes in order to dream?

Paris, February

I take no great pleasure in seeing other people; and I feel that they know this all too well.

Why do I let T*** lure me into talking about my travels? Of course, he *understands* whatever I bring back . . .
He has no thirst for it.

Cuverville, July

Today I reread my travel notes. Publish them—for whom? They will be like those resinous secretions which yield their perfume only when warmed by the hand holding them.

Cuverville, August

I love midsummer, the sun's violent peace. I love this noon hour, when the morning's shrill songs give way to a prostration in the fields and over the mown expanse the air vibrates, and in the scorching furrow the meadowlark stretches its wings. I have walked in the stifling woods, inhaling the scent of the ferns—I have walked to the edge of the woods, I have walked till evening.

I love the smell of the delightful evening, the shade of the haystacks, the sea mist which, in our region, often rises just when the sun is setting, and which spreads, moistens the plain, and before nightfall sheds a comfort in the air, with a sudden chill.

What do you still long for, exigent heart, tireless heart?

. . . On these hot days, I dream of the nomads' freedom . . . Ah, to stay here, yet to run away! Ah, to evaporate, be rid of oneself, so that one blue breath, in which I am dissolved, might journey on . . . !

Tonight, once I was back in my room, I heard through my open window the cries of the nearby harvesters, who now that the reaping is over are at last returning to their village. In a cart, the women and children, half asleep in the straw; the men walk alongside. Everyone is drunk. Their songs are no more than bellowing. Occasionally a louder one—that of the sea conch, the only instrument they know how to use. How many times, in other years, hearing these cries on the plain, when they sounded to me like a call, have I run . . . how many times! Is this all that their intoxication can produce? These men are ugly, and their gods are shapeless. Ah, how many times, after running toward them, have I turned back, disgusted, almost in tears . . .

Tonight, once again, these songs lure me.

Late September

The water in the wadi was so warm it was sheer delight to swim there. Diving in, at first you felt scarcely less sweltering than the air; but its warmth was even, and soon became gentle; then, when you came out, the air, on your wet skin, seemed cool. Then we plunged back in. Then we lay in the sun, stretched out to its rays; then in the shade; it was as cool as in the evenings. —O gaping garments of the Arabs! . . .

Companion! Companion! —Comrade! In Normandy's autumn, I dream of the desert spring.

The rattle of the palm fronds! Almond trees humming with bees! Hot winds, and the sugary savor of the air! . . .

The squalling north wind beats against my windows. It has been raining for three days. —Oh! how lovely the caravans were those evenings in Touggourt, when the sun was sinking into the salt.

TRANSLATOR'S
AFTERWORD

Written over a seven-year period, these four little texts, ranging from an initial Loti-like incantation to the disenchanted scrutiny we recognize nowadays in the "travel writing" of a Naipaul, constitute a sort of hinge in Gide's career, for they mark—under a name borrowed from the Theocritan canon, later assigned by Virgil to a shepherd of enterprising but melancholy eros—an articulation of consciousness: *Amyntas,* far from being a merely decorative opuscule whose rhapsodies have hitherto evaded translation and even commentary because of their submersion in *couleur locale et exotique,* actually accounts for how the author of *The Fruits of the Earth* (1897), that Nietzschean apostrophe to hedonist liberation, even *from* hedonist liberation, becomes the author of *Corydon,* those insistently subversive dialogues on the nature of human sexuality and on the place of the homosexual in society. Gide began writing *Corydon* as soon as *Amyntas* was published, and was to aspire to a preface for this "second shepherd's play"

from Freud himself, an authority scarcely to be invoked
when we think of the first twenty-five or so of Gide's works.

Amyntas, then, is a work of disintoxication, in which
Gide attempts to separate himself—ruefully, gingerly—
from that commitment to Maghrebi prospects and panora-
mas which had hitherto comprised his entire erotic projec-
tion. Of course, he was working in a great French
convention—Flaubert and Fromentin, Delacroix and Loti
had shown him the way, yet only Gide had achieved quite
the tonality of eros in his ecstatic dedication to certain
landscapes, certain desolations of weather and light. Perhaps Gide's commitment, his ardor was so tenacious precisely because the desert is the one place where a man's
thirst cannot be quenched.

Yet in *Amyntas,* the stupefying rhetoric of exoticism
collapses, the identification with a certain "primitive" languor falters. The book is the secret narrative of one more
impoverishment, a destitution which will lead the author to
his authentic riches, his characteristic fictions: *Lafcadio's
Adventures, The Counterfeiters . . .* A structure of exorcism
is perhaps the one constant we can trace in this meta-
morphic career: from his very first work, *The Notebooks and
Poems of André Walter,* published before he was twenty,
Gide was concerned to wrench himself from his comforts,
to chronicle his lacerations thereupon, and to accept no
easy solace. André Walter, like Malte Laurids Brigge (frag-

ments of whose diaries Gide was to translate in 1911), would commit suicide, while Gide, like Rilke, would survive into a new realism, a new reality. By tracing the decline of the substitutive persona, Gide managed to save himself, as did Rilke, for an address to any future revelation; to become, as he put it early on, the most irreplaceable of beings.

It was not easy. The disappointments of the insistently returning lover—the connoisseur of landscape, of *Stimmung*—are bitter, sometimes comical in the chronicling, but they are undergone here for the sake of grander claims, the intimations of a more active eros—adulthood! Indeed, the reader of *Fruits of the Earth* is adjured to throw away that book: its message is in its transcending. An evangel of giving over, the modest *Amyntas* is an enactment of just that manumission; hence it ends in the Normandy autumn, the Gidean persona racked by his longing for that discarded polymorphous perversity he had once discovered for himself *from Biskra to Touggourt.* The opposite of a neurosis, Freud was to say, is a perversion. So Gide was to discover, and *Amyntas* represents the lyrical working-out of that maturation which I should call *barbarism and its discontents* if I had not already called it, when I accompanied the agonized explorer upon his renunciation, *Gide's Way.*

RICHARD HOWARD